THE BOOK OF PHILEMON

Expositor's Study and Commentary

Dr. Maxwell Shimba

Copyright © 2023 – Dr. Maxwell Shimba

All rights reserved. No portion of this book may be reproduced, stored in a retrieval system, or transmitted in any form or by any means – electronics, mechanical, photocopy, recording, scanning, or other – except for brief quotations in critical reviews or articles, without the prior written permission of the publisher.

Published in Manhattan, New York by Shimba Publishing, LLC.

Scripture quotations are from THE NEW KING JAMES VERSION. Copyright © 1982
Used by permission. All rights reserved.

The Scripture quotation noted KJV is from KING JAMES VERSION of the Bible.

Printed in the United States of America

Shimba Publishing LLC

Printed in the United States of America

First Printing Edition 2023

In summary, Onesimus was a fugitive slave who had broken both Jewish and Roman laws by running away from his master. Yet he is mentioned in Scripture as "our beloved brother" (Philemon 1:16) because God had changed him into a new creature; he had been born again through faith in Christ Jesus.

Table of Contents

WHO IS APOSTLE PAUL?

Biography of Apostle Paul

Introduction

Paul, excellent Missionary, Writer and a Theologian of the early Church, is an important figure in the New Testament and also in the history of Christianity. He wrote 13 epistles that comprises about one-fourth of the New Testament. Almost 16 chapters of the book of Acts (13-28) focus on his missionary work.

Birth and Family Background

Paul who used to be called Saul according to history was born in an Asian city known as Tarsus of Cilicia as found in the book of Acts 22:3, which is found in the present-day southern coast of Turkey. One of its important cities was Tarsus. His family was of the tribe of Benjamin and he was named for the most prominent member of the tribe, King Saul. His parents were strict Pharisees due to their strong Jewish background. They were also Roman citizens. It is important to note that even though Judea was within the Roman Empire, most Jews were not Roman citizens. Citizenship outside Roman Empire was an honor reserved for people who made great contributions to the Empire. However, many speculate that Paul's father or grandfather was honored with citizenship because of some special service rendered, thus we may presume that Paul's parents were people of influence and perhaps even moderately wealthy.

Rabbinic Training

At the age of fourteen Paul was sent to Jerusalem to be trained as a Rabbi (Acts 22:3) Paul was fortunate to have under studied a renowned, well-educated and prominent Rabbi known as Gamaliel. At that time Rabbis were taught another trade. The idea was to keep them from becoming a burden on society. They also wanted to have something to fall on during hard times. Paul was not an exception. He was trained to be a tent-maker.

Persecution of Christians

Paul grew to be a man of firm convictions and fiery personality. He always acted on his beliefs. Thus, when he was confronted with what he took to be a heresy to Judaism, he worked with all his might to quell it. This heresy would one day come to be known as Christianity and Paul was among the foremost of its persecutors. A very good example is when Stephen was being stoned. Paul was present. Although he did not participate, he encouraged the violent act that destroyed the first of the martyrs. He then participated in a general persecution including, ''going from house to house, he dragged out the believers, both men and women and threw them into jail.''

Paul's Conversion

He then undertook a mission to Damascus. There he intended to continue attacking Christians. However, on the way, he had a vision. This vision is described several times in the Bible, three times in the book of Acts. Paul saw Jesus who asked why Paul persisted in persecuting Him. He then commissioned Paul to preach His message to the Gentiles.

This meeting with Jesus made Paul a Christian. Even so, Paul always insisted that he remained both a Jew and a Roman. But before he could fully accept this message from Jesus, Paul spent some time in Arabia and then Damascus. Searching his soul, he undertook the mission he believed had been given to him directly by Jesus. He preached in Damascus for three years. His enemies were determined to kill him so he had to slip out of the city by night.

Paul's Missionary Journey

He went to Jerusalem and there gained official sanction from the elders of the Church, including Peter and James, to bring the message of Jesus to the Gentiles. Along with Barnabas, he then went on his first Missionary Journey to Cyprus, Antioch in Pisidia,

Iconium, Lystra and Derbe. During this journey they met many hardships. Paul was even stoned, though not killed, in Lystra. It was an ironic twist that Paul underwent the same gruesome punishment he had sanctioned for Stephen and for the very cause Stephen had suffered.

Around 50 A.D. he returned to Jerusalem to report to the church elders. His visit provoked a dispute over whether Christians had to first become Jews. Paul said no. The controversy was temporarily resolved in his favor and he went on his second and third missionary journeys to Galatia, Phrygia, Macedonia and Greece. He even went to Athens where he argued with philosophers as well as pagans.

It was during this period that he met Luke, a doctor who would become a close adherent and would eventually write one of the gospels as well as the book of Acts. After his third missionary journey, Paul returned to Jerusalem where he ran into a dispute with the Sanhedrin. He was the object of a huge civil disturbance. For this, he was arrested and eventually brought to Caesarea.

While there, he was questioned and tried several times, but his enemies could not seem to make their charges stick. Even so, he was held by the governor, Felix, who was afraid he might again create problems in Jerusalem. The next governor, Festus, seemed to be loath to come to a decision on his case, so after over two years of house arrest, Paul invoked his right as a Roman citizen to demand a trial before the Emperor.

He was sent on the next ship to Rome. However, the ship met heavy seas and wrecked on the Island of Malta. Paul prayed and was visited by an Angel and the entire crew was saved. Paul eventually took another boat and reached Italy. He was met by supporters and eventually made it to Rome.

Paul's final years

It is known that he spent at least two years under house arrest waiting his audience with Nero. Extant literature close to the time indicates that Paul was either tried or executed by the sword or he died during the persecution that came about after the great fire where Nero was reputed to have incited the blaze and to have fiddled during the conflagration in about 64 AD. Some tradition also has it that Paul escaped the persecution and went on to continue his preaching in Spain. Whatever his end, it is certain that Paul was a great influence on modern Christianity, both through his missionary work and his writing.

Apostle Paul's contribution to Christianity

It has been said that if it were not for Paul and a few others such as Barnabas that Christianity would have remained a small unknown branch of Judaism. Paul was the leading missionary to the Gentiles (Non-Jewish). While many within the early church were determined that a Christian must first become a Jew, Paul insisted that this was not the case. He recognized that the message of Jesus was for all men. In a letter to the Galatians, he thoroughly spelled out a case for the message of Jesus being a ''New Covenant'' with humanity.

According to Paul, Abraham accepted God of his free will, and God favored Abraham for this reason. This was the covenant that God made with Abraham and his descendants. The laws given to Moses were not set down for another couple hundred years. So, Paul believed that they were not part of the original bargain, but were given later to Moses as an intermediate guide until Jesus came to set down the new ''Law'' and the New ''Covenant''.

Paul noted that Jesus died on the Cross not only for our sins, but to take on the burden of Mosaic Law. Thus, a Christian need not first become a Jew in order to follow Jesus. This was revealed when he commented that like Abraham Christians are saved by their faith alone. The zeal Paul used to persecute Christians was changed. He did all that he could to discourage the issue of separating Jews from Gentiles by means of his vivid interpretation of the word of God to the various churches. Paul, himself, seems to have been of the opinion that faith was all that was required.

He succeeded in making Christianity a universal religion, not just in the spiritual sense but also in the physical sense. Spreading the Gospel far and wide across the Roman Empire was

Paul's mission. His missionary journeys brought him to Asia Minor, Greece, Macedonia and eventually Rome.

There is no question that his Roman citizenship and his intense training as a Pharisee helped him immensely in this mission. He was arrested several times because of his preaching and several times was saved because of his elevated status within the Empire.

Besides being a fiery orator, Paul was also a capable writer. His letters make up the bulk of the epistles in the Bible. Because his writings were so treasured, they are among the most studied today. The words of Paul carry weight far greater than those of James or Peter, some of whose letters also survive. Paul's thoughtfulness, gentleness and steadfastness infuse his letters and they also infuse the close adherents of his words today.

Paul was a charismatic individual. He was a sure leader of men. Seldom did he doubt himself. He saw his mission as not only bringing the "Good News" to the Gentiles, but also to organize the Church so that it would grow, even when he was not present to urge it on. Thus, he created an organization and trained leaders. This organization would one day become modern Christianity as it came to supersede the original authority of the Church in Jerusalem.

Conclusion

Paul was vitally shaped by a dramatic meeting with Christ on the Road to Damascus and it was this drama, coupled with his fervor that would mold Christianity for the next millennia. Christians today see Christ somewhat through the prism of Paul's teaching.

Ultimately, it was Paul who both physically and theologically made Christianity a ''universal'' church. More importantly, the appendix to the teachings of the Gospel, the Epistles of the Apostle Paul should be the subject of an attentive and earnest study of every person that seeks a deeper understanding of the Christian faith. These Epistles are outstanding in their remarkably elevated religious thoughts, reflecting the Apostle Paul's extensive knowledge and scholarship of the Old Testament, which were equal to his profound understanding of Christ's New Testament teachings.

The Acts of the Apostles is an original source that largely chronicles Paul's life. It is thought by some scholars that the book may even have been a legal brief based on the recollections of Paul and the diary of Luke to help serve in his defense during his trial before the Emperor. Interestingly, neither the book of Acts nor Paul's surviving letters depicts the results of Paul's trial.

INTRODUCTION

John 14:26
New American Standard Bible
But the Helper, the Holy Spirit whom the Father will send in My name, He will teach you all things, and remind you of all that I said to you.

The Holy Spirit is our helper. He teaches us day after day and night after night. How can we fail with this very powerful being living inside of us, directing us and guiding us? Our job is to listen and take His advice and obey God's commands.

For more than two years while in Ephesus during his commission, Apostle Paul ministered in Asia Minor. This was a successful period for the apostle to the Gentiles, who saw many converts among both residents of Ephesus and visitors to the city. One of the people converted under Paul's teaching pursuant to the Book of Philemon 1:19 was a man called Philemon, a slaveowner from the nearby city of Colossae. In the Infallible Word, the book that bears Philemon's name, Paul addressed his "beloved brother" as a "fellow worker," a title given to those who served for a time alongside Paul. The two gospel writers Mark and Luke also received this title later in the letter as impeccably exhibited in Philemon 1:1, 24. Conspicuously, a kinship existed between Paul and Philemon, one that would serve a significant purpose in light of the circumstance that brought about the letter.

As a counselor, I have walked the road of frustration with several clients whose issues were a result of inadequate life skills. There are two great steps in helping the client deal with the issues that precede obtaining necessary life skills. First, help the client recover from the shame or embarrassment that often accompanies this deficit. Second, help the client find empathy and forgiveness for parents or guardians who had inadequate skills to pass on or who were too busy to make training a priority. The process of removing emotional roadblocks and obtaining the missing skill set will take humility and patience. However, for your clients, this process could mean the difference between being the initiator of frustration to all who fall under their leadership and being a confident leader in their realms of responsibility.

Romans 12:2 Do not conform to the pattern of this world, but be transformed by the renewing of your mind. Then you will be able to test and approve what God's will is—his good, pleasing and perfect will. The work of the Holy Ghost first begins in the understanding, and is carried on to the will, affections, and conversation, till there is a change of the whole man into the likeness of God, in knowledge, righteousness, and true holiness. Thus, to be godly, is to give up ourselves to God.

This verse warns us that the "world system," the popular culture and manner of thinking that is in rebellion against God, will try to conform us to its ungodly pattern, and that process must be resisted. The battle ground between conforming to the world and being transformed is within the mind of the believer. Christians must think differently.

Accordingly, Paul made a request. He wanted Philemon to forgive a runaway slave, Onesimus, and receive him as a brother in Christ, as the apostle found him useful in God's service pursuant to Philemon 1:11–14. Paul did not minimize Onesimus's sin, however, there was sacrifice required in this request, and because of that, Apostle Paul approached the request with gentleness and care as exhibited in Philemon 1:21. His letter to Philemon vividly presents the beautiful and majestic transition from slavery to kinship that comes as a result of Christian love and forgiveness. The Bible says, "Bear with each other and forgive one another if any of you has a grievance against someone. Forgive as the Lord forgave you".

DR. MAXWELL SHIMBA

CHAPTER I

Who Is the Author of This Epistle?

Philemon 1:1 Expositor's Study:

"Paul, a prisoner of Jesus Christ, and Timothy our brother, unto Philemon our dearly beloved, and fellow labourer, and to our beloved Apphia, and Archippus our fellow soldier, and to the church in thy house: Grace to you, and peace, from God our Father and the Lord Jesus Christ" (Philemon 1-3).

Who is the author of this epistle?

This is a personal letter from the Apostle Paul to Philemon, a wealthy Christian from Colossae.

This very heart-warming letter was written by Paul for the purpose of interceding for the runaway slave who had become a faithful Christian around AD 60-62. He not only was pleading for mercy for him from his master, Philemon - he was also reminding Philemon of his duty as a fellow Christian toward this man. It was also intended for reading to the entire church that met in Philemon's home.

The descriptive title the author gave himself in verse 1 is a prisoner of Jesus Christ because Paul did not consider himself a prisoner of Rome, or of circumstances, or of the religious leaders who had stirred up his legal troubles (Acts 23-24). Paul always counted himself to be a prisoner of Jesus Christ.

Theme:

The theme of Paul's letter to Philemon is the power of the gospel to transform individual lives (v. 11) and human relationships (v. 16). Onesimus had experienced that transforming power in his life ("formerly he was useless" but "now he is indeed useful"; v. 11). Paul therefore urged his friend Philemon to form a new relationship with Onesimus, his runaway slave.

This letter was written while Paul was in prison in Rome. This is the reason for his comment in opening the letter that he is, "a prisoner of Jesus Christ." He knew by experience that no bars could hold him if it was not the will of God that he should remain where he was.

First Paul was arrested by the Roman authorities in Jerusalem after the Jews started a murderous riot because of his presence there. They accused him of being" ... the man, that teacheth all men everywhere against the people, and the law, and this place (Acts 21:28).

Paul was sent to Rome after he exercised his legal right as a Roman citizen to appeal his case to Caesar (Acts 26:32). After an extremely dangerous voyage across The Mediterranean Sea that included a shipwreck on Malta, Paul finally arrived in Rome (Acts 28:16).

Below is a list of 3 verses in this epistle where Paul referred to his imprisonment.:

a): Philemon 1:1
b): Philemon 1:9
c): Philemon 1:10

The Book of Philemon is one of the 4 "prison epistles. The other 3 epistles that were written from a prison cell are:

a): Philippians
b): Ephesians
c): Colossians

Paul remained in Rome for at least two years (Acts 28:30), where, despite being a prisoner, he wrote several epistles. Some commentators believe the epistle to Philemon was Paul's first epistle written from prison. It is also believed the epistles to the Colossians and Ephesians were written about the same time as Philemon.

Paul didn't consider being in prison an inconvenience because he knew that he was "a prisoner of Jesus Christ." He knew by experience that no bars could hold him if it was not the will of God that he should remain where he was.

Although the Bible does not tell us how this imprisonment ended, most scholars believe that he was eventually acquitted of the charges and released in 63 or 64 A.D. After being released, he made his way back through Greece and Asia Minor (i.e. Turkey) before again being arrested and returned to Rome where he was martyred about 67 A.D.

What did Paul confess when he gave his testimony to King Agrippa in Acts 26:9-11?

His conscience kept his failures. Exhibit: *When he gave testimony to King Agrippa, he said, "I verily thought with myself, that I ought to do many things contrary to the name of Jesus of Nazareth. Which thing I also did in Jerusalem: and many of the saints did I shut up in prison, having received authority from the chief priests; and when they were put to death, I gave my voice against them. And I punished them oft in every synagogue, and compelled them to blaspheme; and being exceedingly mad against them, I persecuted them even unto strange cities" (Acts 26:9-11).*

Paul spoke of the great regret he had over his former life as a persecutor (1 Corinthians 15:9, 1 Timothy 1:15). Maybe the fact that he tried to force them to blaspheme weighed most heavily on his conscience.

In this verse, he also said, " I cast my vote against them." This implies that Paul was a member of the Sanhedrin, and officially voted against Christians who were tried before the Sanhedrin (as Stephen was in Acts 7).

Paul considered himself a prisoner of debt because he could never have paid or earned his way to forgiveness.

There was no part of Paul's life in which he was not a prisoner. In those days, the ancient Jews commonly referred to the yoke to express someone's obligation to God. There was the yoke of the kingdom, the yoke of the law, the yoke of the command, the yoke of repentance, the yoke of faith, and the general yoke of God. In this context, it is easy to see why Paul had ... (Matthew 11:29): to take his yoke upon Jesus. He belonged to his Master, his Redeemer.

People of that time would understand this analogy better than we do today. When training a new animal (such as an ox) to plow, ancient farmers often yoked it to an older, stronger, more experienced animal who bore the burden and guided the young animal through the learning process. In addition, the yoke was carefully adjusted, so that it would fit well, and not rub or hurt the neck of the animal. The yoke was tailor-made to fit the ox.

Jesus said it plainly, "My yoke is easy and My burden is light." If the person you are counseling complains that his yoke is too hard and his burden is too heavy to bear, then we can say with confidence that this person isn't letting Jesus bear it with him.

After Paul came to know the Lord, his entire life was given to the service of Jesus Christ.

Who was present when Paul wrote the epistle to the Colossians? (Colossians 1:1): Timotheus

Timothy was an honored companion of Paul, but he was not an apostle. Although Timothy is included in this salutation, he did not have any part in composing this epistle. Some commentators say he may have served as a scribe for the apostle.

Philemon 1:1 Commentary:

The Book of Philemon is a brief yet profound letter within the New Testament, attributed to the apostle Paul. This epistle is distinct in that it is a personal letter addressing a specific situation and offering insights into Christian ethics, reconciliation, and the transformative power of the gospel. The opening verse, Philemon 1:1, provides a concise introduction to the themes and characters central to the letter.

"Paul, a prisoner for Christ Jesus, and Timothy our brother, To Philemon our beloved fellow worker:"

The verse begins with the author's identification: "Paul, a prisoner for Christ Jesus." Here, the apostle Paul introduces himself not merely as a prisoner of earthly authorities but as a captive for the cause of Christ. This self-designation underscores his unwavering commitment to Christ's mission, even in the face of adversity. Paul's use of "prisoner" reveals the sacrifices he has made for the spread of the gospel.

The mention of Timothy as "our brother" emphasizes the close bond between Paul and his co-worker. Timothy's association with Paul suggests their shared dedication to Christ's work and mutual affection as believers. This camaraderie exemplifies the interconnectedness of the early Christian community and the collaborative nature of their ministry.

The intended recipient of the letter is introduced next: "To Philemon our beloved fellow worker." Philemon is characterized as a "beloved fellow worker," highlighting his active involvement in the propagation of the gospel and his close relationship with Paul. The term "fellow worker" signifies more than mere camaraderie; it implies a shared commitment to advancing God's kingdom. Philemon's role in the spread of the gospel is acknowledged, underscoring the importance of every believer's contribution to the mission.

Key Themes and Implications:

This verse lays the foundation for the overarching themes explored in the Book of Philemon:

1. Suffering for Christ: Paul's identification as a "prisoner for Christ Jesus" introduces the theme of suffering for the sake of the gospel. This theme serves as a backdrop for the subsequent discussions on forgiveness, reconciliation, and selflessness.

2. Christian Brotherhood: The reference to Timothy as "our brother" emphasizes the spiritual kinship among believers. It highlights the importance of unity, support, and collaboration within the Christian community.

3. Beloved Fellow Worker: Philemon's title as a "beloved fellow worker" underscores the value of every individual's contribution to the body of Christ. This theme promotes a

sense of purpose and responsibility among believers, irrespective of their societal roles.

4. Personal Relationships and Transformation: The choice of addressing Philemon directly indicates the personal nature of the letter. The subsequent verses reveal that the letter centers around the matter of Onesimus, Philemon's runaway slave. The transformation of Onesimus through his encounter with Paul and the gospel becomes a powerful illustration of the redemptive and transformative nature of Christianity.

In conclusion, Philemon 1:1 serves as an introductory glimpse into the letter's broader themes of suffering, unity, and transformation. The apostle Paul's self-identification as a prisoner for Christ Jesus, the mention of Timothy as a brother, and the characterization of Philemon as a beloved fellow worker all contribute to setting the stage for the subsequent exploration of forgiveness, reconciliation, and the radical impact of the gospel on personal relationships and societal norms. The letter's enduring relevance lies in its teachings on love, mercy, and the transcendent power of Christ's message to shape lives and communities.

Study and Discussion Guide Verse 1:

1. Who is the author of this epistle?
2. What descriptive title did the author give himself in verse 1?
3. Where was Paul when he wrote the letter? Name the city and location within the city.:
4. List the 3 verses in this epistle where Paul referred to his imprisonment.:
a):
b):
c):
5. Philemon is one of the 4 "prison epistles." Research to find out the other 3 epistles that were written from a prison cell.:
a):
b):
c):

6. Why didn't Paul consider being in prison an inconvenience?

7. The author of our accompaniment text says that Paul was a prisoner in more than one sense.:

a) Paul was a prisoner of ...:

b) Paul was a prisoner of ...:

c) Paul was a prisoner of

d) Paul was a prisoner of ...:

8. What did Paul confess when he gave his testimony to King Agrippa in Acts 26:9-11?

9. Paul considered himself a prisoner of debt because he could never have paid or earned his way to ______.:

10. There was no part of Paul's life in which he was not a prisoner. In those days, the ancient Jews commonly referred to the yoke to express someone's obligation to God. There was the yoke of the kingdom, the yoke of the law, the yoke of the command, the yoke of repentance, the yoke of faith, and the general yoke of God. In this context, it is easy to see why Paul had ... (Matthew 11:29):

11. After Paul came to know the Lord, his entire life was given to the service of ______,

12. Who was present when Paul wrote the epistle to the Colossians? (Colossians 1:1):

CHAPTER II

A Letter Addressed to Philemon, Apphia and Archippus

Philemon 1:2 Expositor's Study:

Philemon 1:2 also to Apphia our sister and Archippus our fellow soldier—and to the church that meets in your home:

This letter was addressed to Philemon, Apphia and Archippus as exhibited in verses 1 and 2.:

Note: Baker's Pictorial Introduction to the Bible by William S. Deal says that Apphia was Philemon's wife, and Archippus was their son.

Because Archippus' name was included in the salutation, we can surmise that all three were members of the Church at Laodicea. (Colossians 4:17).

Although there were 3 names included in the salutation, it is evident that the letter was primarily directed toward Philemon a beloved friend and fellow laborer with Paul. By mentioning the others, it may be that Paul was soliciting their help in encouraging this man regarding the situation he was about to address that required kindness and forgiveness.

We know Philemon must have been wealthy, because he owned slaves, including Onesimus, and because his house was so big that they could hold church services there. Now this was probably just a small group from the Colossian church, rather than the entire membership.

Philemon's benevolence and generosity toward his fellow Christians is brought out in verses 5 through 7. Also, he was known for his hospitality, and we know Paul was aware of this since, in verse 22, he asked if he could come for an overnight visit when he got out of prison.

Tradition says that Apphia was the wife of Philemon, and Archippus was their son. What a good example of this family's devotion to Christ and of their hospitality to the saints that we see in this verse, they had love and faith toward Jesus Christ and toward all saints.

For hundreds of years now, the idea of the church has been almost universally associated with a church building. Even though biblically informed Christians know that the church is made up of people, not a building, it remains almost impossible for some to escape the association between a particular local church and the building in which that church gathers.

But the earliest Christians felt no need to construct special buildings for their gatherings. No church building, as such, can be identified until at least the end of the second century, and the grand, ornate structures that marked the Middle Ages did not become the norm until the fourth century — the time of the Roman emperor Constantine. The first Christians met wherever they could, the most popular setting being in private homes.

Verses that make note of the early believers' meeting in private homes include:
- Acts 2:46
- Acts 5:42
- Romans 16:5
- Romans 16:23

- 1 Corinthians 16:19
- Colossians 4:15
- Philemon 1:2

What we learn about Philemon from the information shared in this epistle in verse 1 is that Philemon was dearly beloved and fellow labourer.

Paul called Philemon a fellow-laborer, so he most likely held some office in the church at Colossae. The Bible doesn't tell us if he was a presbyter or simply a reader or usher, but title also implies that Philemon took part in the work of spreading the gospel.

From the following verses we learn that:

Verse 2: Philemon had a Church in his house.

Verse 5: Philemon had love and faith toward the Lord Jesus, and toward all saints

Verse 6: Philemon was a good person and had faith in Jesus

Verse 15-16: Philemon had a servant called Onesimus and was asked to receive him back as a brother beloved.

And in verse 19 we learn that Philemon must have been converted by Paul. Paul said he owed his salvation to him. The relationship between Paul and Philemon was so close and so intimate that Paul didn't hesitate to pressure him, on the basis of it, to forgive his slave, Onesimus, for stealing from him and running away.

Tradition says that Philemon later became the bishop of Colossae, and that he, together with his wife and son and Onesimus, were martyred by stoning before Androcles, the governor, in the days of Nero. However, this is not revealed in the Scriptures, so to know for sure - we will just have to ask him about it when we get to heaven.

Philemon 1:2 Commentary:

The second verse of the Book of Philemon may appear brief, but it contains significant insights into the nature of Christian relationships and the expression of grace within the community of believers. While it serves as part of the opening salutation, it unveils layers of meaning that contribute to the overarching themes of the letter.

".. and Apphia our sister and Archippus our fellow soldier, and the church in your house:"

In this verse, the apostle Paul extends his greetings to additional individuals within the Christian community associated with Philemon:

1. Apphia our sister: The mention of Apphia as "our sister" underscores the familial bond that characterizes the relationships among believers. This designation emphasizes the spiritual unity and equality that exist among all followers of Christ, regardless of gender or societal roles. The term "sister" signifies the shared identity and shared purpose that comes with being part of the body of Christ. It's a reminder that the Christian community is a family bound by the love of Christ.

2. Archippus our fellow soldier: Archippus is described as a "fellow soldier," highlighting the spiritual battle that believers engage in as they live out their faith. This imagery suggests that the Christian journey involves both challenges and victories. Archippus is recognized for his active involvement in the mission of Christ, just as a soldier is dedicated to a cause. This term also implies a call to action, urging Archippus to fulfill his role in the ongoing spiritual warfare.

3. The church in your house: This phrase provides a glimpse into the early structure of Christian gatherings. It reveals that Philemon's house served as a place of worship and fellowship for local believers. This intimate setting is reminiscent of the early gatherings of Christians in homes, where they would come together for worship, teaching, prayer, and mutual support. This reference highlights the

importance of hospitality and the role that individual households played in nurturing the growth of the early church.

Key Themes and Implications:

Philemon 1:2 introduces several key themes and implications that echo throughout the letter:

1. Community and Fellowship: The inclusion of Apphia and Archippus, along with the mention of the church in Philemon's house, underscores the communal nature of the Christian faith. It highlights the importance of relationships and the sense of belonging that comes from being part of a faith community.

2. Spiritual Unity: The terms "sister" and "fellow soldier" emphasize the spiritual unity that transcends social and gender distinctions. The language Paul employs promotes a sense of shared purpose, mutual support, and collaboration among believers.

3. Domestic Worship: The reference to the church meeting in Philemon's house emphasizes the simplicity and inclusivity of early Christian gatherings. It reminds us that faith is not confined to formal institutions but can thrive in the everyday settings of believers' lives.

4. Responsibility and Calling: Describing Archippus as a "fellow soldier" underscore the idea that every believer has a unique role and calling within the body of Christ. This theme encourages individual believers to actively engage in the work of the gospel, fulfilling their God-given responsibilities.

In summary, Philemon 1:2 may be a concise verse, but it provides a window into the rich tapestry of relationships, roles, and responsibilities within the early Christian community. Through the greetings extended to Apphia, Archippus, and the church in Philemon's house, Paul lays the groundwork for the themes of unity, shared purpose, and individual calling that are explored in greater depth in the rest of the letter. The verse serves as a reminder that the Christian faith is not just a personal journey but a collective endeavor, where each member contributes to the growth and impact of the body of Christ.

Study and Discussion Guide Verse 2:

1. List all the church members to whom this letter was addressed in verses 1 and 2.:
a):
b):
c):
2. Because Archippus' name was included in the salutation, we can surmise that all three were members of the church at ______. (Colossians 4:17):
3. Although there were 3 names included in the salutation, it is evident that the letter was primarily directed toward ______, a beloved friend and fellow laborer with Paul. By mentioning the others, it may be that Paul was soliciting their help in encouraging this man regarding the situation he was about to address that required kindness and forgiveness.:
4. Tradition says that Apphia was the wife of Philemon, and Archippus was their son. What is a good example of this family's devotion to Christ and of their hospitality to the saints that we see in this verse?
5. What can we learn about Philemon from the information shared in this epistle?

a)   vs.   1:
b)   vs.   2:
c)   vs.   5:
d)   vs.   6:
e)   vs.   15-
16:

CHAPTER III

Two Blessings Mentioned in Verse 3

Philemon 1:3 Expositor's Study:

Philemon 1:3 Grace to you and peace from God our Father and the Lord Jesus Christ.

You should note that there are two blessings mentioned in verse 3. Paul prays this church would enjoy:

a): Grace

b): Peace

Grace must come first if we are to have true peace.

This was Paul's customary greeting, found in each one of his letters. However, normally the greeting was extended to the entire congregation. In this epistle, the greeting was directed to Philemon as an individual. This makes the letter unique among Paul's writings.

The other Pastoral Epistles (1 and 2 Timothy and Titus) are also written first to individuals, but the character of their content suggests that they were intended to be shared with the entire congregation. Philemon really is a personal note written by Paul to one man.

Note: The significance of the order in which these two blessings are named. From God our Father and the Lord Jesus Christ.

In verse 3 we learn that Paul says these blessings would flow from:

a): God the Father

b): Lord Jesus Christ

What person of the Trinity is not mentioned here in Verse 3?

Holy Spirit

Frequently, when the apostles—especially Paul—referred to the God Family in the greeting of their writings, mention of the Holy Spirit is absent. See James 1:1; II Peter 1:2; I John 1:3; Romans 1:7; I Corinthians 1:3; II Corinthians 1:2; Galatians 1:3; Ephesians 1:2; Philippians 1:2; Colossians 1:2; I Thessalonians 1:1; II Thessalonians 1:2; I Timothy 1:1-2; II Timothy 1:2; Titus 1:4; and our scripture here - Philemon 1:3.

What are some of the jobs and functions of the 3rd Person of the Trinity?

a) John 16:8: He will reprove the world of sin, and of righteousness, and of judgment:

Men cannot come to an understanding of sin, righteousness and judgment apart from the Holy Spirit. In its insanity, the world regarded Jesus as a sinner, itself as righteous, and it ended up pronouncing false judgment on Jesus Himself.

b) John 16:13: He will guide you into all truth.

c) Titus 3:5: Washing of regeneration and renewing

d) John 15:26; 16:14: He shall testify and glorify Jesus.

e) Acts 9:31: Comfort the Church.

f) Acts 20:28; 13:2: Holy Ghost hath made us overseers, to feed the church of God, which he hath purchased with his own blood. The Holy Ghost has called us.

g) Romans 8:14; Galatians 5:18; Matthew 4:1; Luke 4:1: The Holy Ghost will lead us.

Apostle Paul didn't say, "As many as go to church, these are the sons of God." And he didn't say, "As many as read their Bibles, these are the sons of God." Although we may take all the right steps to be led by the Spirit, we really need to inspect the fruit in our lives to be sure. Following are signs that will indicate we are truly being led by the Holy Spirit.

If I am being led by the Spirit …

- I'll live a life of righteousness. (Psalm 5:8) The Holy Spirit's leading always results in a life of righteousness. If sin is the result of the guidance that I've received and followed, then either it wasn't the Holy Spirit's leading, or else I didn't follow His leading as I should have.
- I'll live a life led by the Bible and its principles. (Psalm 25:5) The Bible is God's truth, given by inspiration of the Holy Spirit, and the Holy Spirit will always lead us into the truth of the Bible.
- I'll live a life led in a plain path. (Psalm 27:11) A plain path is a straight, level, well-traveled road, without any hidden snares or traps or places where the enemy can hide and ambush us. And although the devil will always try to trip us up, the path we travel won't contribute to Satan's work in our lives.
- I'll live a life glorifying to God. (Psalm 31:3) When God is leading us, He does it in a way that brings glory to Himself, rather than to us. God guides us for His Name's sake, with the motive of glorifying Himself, not us.
- I'll live a life of assurance. (Psalm 139:24) When we live by faith, God gives us the blessed inward assurance of that eternal life we received when we accepted Jesus Christ as our Savior and Lord.
- I'll live a life of spiritual safety. (Psalm 78:53) You see, God protects His own when we obey the Spirit's leading in our lives. The plain path is also the safe path.

- I'll live a life of witnessing for Jesus Christ. (Acts 1:8) Jesus told His disciples that the entrance of the Holy Spirit would transform them into witnesses for Christ. And if the Holy Spirit is leading us, the things He leads us to do will be a good testimony for the Lord Jesus Christ.
- *I'll* live a life delivered from evil. (Matthews 6:13) Under the Holy Spirit's guidance, we will be led out of temptation and delivered from Satan's tricks and traps. We may not be able to see what's coming down the pike at us, but the Holy Spirit can, and He leads us away from spiritual harm.
- I'll live a life with my heart fed by God (Psalm 23). When the Holy Spirit leads us, He leads us to the green pastures and deep, still waters of God's Word. If the Spirit has led, we will always be fed.
- I'll live a life led in proper ways. (Isa. 48:17) The Holy Spirit will always lead us in the way that we should go – the proper way, the good way, the right way.
- I'll have a life of peace of soul and spirit. (1 Corinthians 7:15b; 1 Corinthians 14:33; Galatians 5:22) We already have peace with God through our Lord Jesus Christ. But we can also have the peace of God that rule in our hearts when we're led by the Holy Spirit.

h) 2 Thessalonians 2:13; 1 Peter 1:2; Romans 5:16: Sanctification of the Spirit.

i) Acts 1:8, Luke 4:14; 24:49; Romans 15:19: Holy Ghost will give us Power.

j) Ephesians 5:18; Acts 2:4; 4:8, 31; 9:17: We will be filled with the Holy Ghost

k) Romans 8:26: Holy Ghost is our Helper

l) Matthew 12:28: Holy Ghost bring the Kingdom of God to us.

m) 2 Peer 1:21: Holy Ghost will make us prophecy

Holy men speak and prophecy as they are moved by the Holy Spirit. In this verse, the ancient Greek word translated "moved" has the sense of carried along, as a ship being carried along by the wind or the current (the same word is used of a ship in Acts 27:15, 17). It is as if the writers of Scripture "raised their sails" in cooperation with God and the Holy Spirit carried them along in the direction He wished.

n) 1 Thessalonians 1:6: He will make us follower of the Lord Jesus with JOY.

o) Romans 8:16: The Spirit itself beareth witness with our spirit, that we are the children of God.

p) Galatians 5:22-23: But the fruit of the Spirit is love, joy, peace, longsuffering, gentleness, goodness, faith, Meekness, temperance

q) 1 Corinthians 12:1-11: He will give us Spiritual gifts as He will: Exhibit: 1 Corinthians 12:1-11

r) Ephesians 1:13; 4:3: Holy Spirit is our Seal

s) 1 Corinthians 2:11: The Holy Spirit knows the mind of God for He is God.

We could NEVER guess what God is thinking on our own. Here Paul reminds us that only the Holy Spirit can tell us about God and His wisdom.

What a great review about all the things the Holy Spirit does for us.

1. In the world today, one of the best ways to manipulate another person into doing what you want is to ...: Tell people what they want to hear, and talk about how great they are.

I would call this subtle emotional manipulation.

2. In verses 4 through 7, as Paul set the stage for his request, he is ...: being completely sincere in his compliments and praise.

Paul frequently used compliments and praise as a means to encourage and stimulate the people to whom he ministered. He was not a man to flatter people just to gain popularity. His words were sincere expressions of genuine appreciation. If they had done well, then Paul commended them - not in a way to puff them up, but in such a manner as to encourage them to continue in doing well.

Following Paul's example, there are many times when we can help people by a simple word of commendation. A sincere compliment is one of the best encouragements we can give.

In Verse 4, Apostle Paul's thanksgiving for Philemon was Godward, personal, and continual.: It was God he thanked, and to God he prayed. It was Philemon for whom he prayed. If we could remember to pray for those on our hearts as Paul did, we would not have time to scheme and manipulate others for our own purpose. It was God's purpose that held Paul's attention.

Pursuant to Colossians 4:12, Apostle Paul could have heard from Epaphras about what was going on with Philemon, when he himself was in Rome, in prison.

Epaphras was a distinguished disciple, and possibly the founder of the Colossian church. He was with Paul during part of his 1st Roman imprisonment, as we see in verse 23, where he is called by Paul his "fellow-prisoner." Paul's regard for him is shown by his designating him "our beloved fellow-servant," "a faithful minister of Christ" (Colossians 1:7), and "a bondservant of Christ Jesus" (Colossians 4:12).
Paul noticed the good things people did, and always remembered to thank them. Apostle Paul felt led to commend and thank the following Saints:

a) Romans 1:8-9: Saints in Rome

b) 1 Thessalonians 1:2-3: The church in Thessalonica

c) 1 Corinthians 1:4-6: The church of God which is at Corinth

We see that Paul not only thanked the people for what they were doing, but he also let them know that he always makes mention of them in his prayers.

These people had been such a blessing to Paul that Paul prayed for them often and with thanksgiving to God. We should remember to do the same for people who are a blessing in our own lives.

Paul was actually doing exactly what he preached. In Ephesians 6:18 and 1 Timothy 2:1, Paul is telling us to pray always with all prayer and supplication in the Spirit, and watching thereunto with all perseverance and supplication for all saints; Exhibit 1 Timothy 2:1 I exhort therefore, that, first of all, supplications, prayers, intercessions, and giving of thanks, be made for all men;

Following Paul's example who followed Jesus' example, when we are impressed to pray for others, the following are some blessings we might pray that they enjoy:

a) Ephesians 1:17: the spirit of wisdom and revelation in the knowledge of Him.

b) Ephesians 3:16: That he would grant you, according to the riches of his glory, to be strengthened with might by his Spirit in the inner man;

c) Ephesians 3:17: That Christ may dwell in our hearts by faith; that we, being rooted and grounded in love,

Paul prayed that they would KNOW the love of Christ. This is a spiritual reality, but Paul didn't want them to base their knowledge on feelings or emotions, but on the facts as revealed by the Holy Spirit.

d) Philippians 1:9: that our love may abound yet more and more in knowledge and in all judgment;

e) 1 Thessalonians 3:12: And the Lord make you to increase and abound in love one toward another, and toward all men, even as we do toward you

f) 1 Thessalonians 3:13: To the end he may stablish your hearts unblameable in holiness before God, even our Father, at the coming of our Lord Jesus Christ with all his saints.

g) 2 Thessalonians 1:11: Wherefore also we pray always for you, that our God would count you worthy of this calling, and fulfil all the good pleasure of his goodness, and the work of faith with power:

h) 2 Thessalonians 3:5: And the Lord direct your hearts into the love of God, and into the patient waiting for Christ.

Paul undoubtedly had felt God strengthen and protect him, and was confident that He would also help the Thessalonians as they were enduring persecution stirred up by the "evil one" in verse 3.

Philemon 1:3 Commentary:

The third verse of the Book of Philemon provides a glimpse into the apostle Paul's heart and attitude toward Philemon, the recipient of this personal letter. In this verse, Paul expresses gratitude and commendation for Philemon, setting the tone for the themes of love, fellowship, and mutual respect that pervade the rest of the letter.

"Grace to you and peace from God our Father and the Lord Jesus Christ."

In this short but impactful verse, Paul extends a familiar Christian greeting to Philemon: "Grace to you and peace from God our Father and the Lord Jesus Christ." This greeting carries a depth of meaning that speaks to the heart of the Christian faith and sets the stage for the themes to be explored in the letter.

Key Themes and Implications:

1. Grace: The mention of "grace" emphasizes God's unmerited favor and kindness toward believers. By invoking "grace," Paul reminds Philemon of the foundational principle of Christianity: that salvation and reconciliation with God are a result of God's grace extended through the sacrificial death and resurrection of Jesus Christ. This term also hints at the larger theme of forgiveness and reconciliation that will be addressed in the context of Philemon's relationship with Onesimus.

2. Peace: The concept of "peace" carries a sense of wholeness, harmony, and reconciliation. It signifies the peace that believers experience through their relationship with God and the transformative power of Christ's message. This notion of peace also anticipates the eventual appeal Paul will make to Philemon to extend peace and reconciliation toward Onesimus, the runaway slave.

3. God our Father and the Lord Jesus Christ: The reference to "God our Father and the Lord Jesus Christ" underscores the Trinitarian nature of the Christian faith. It highlights the believers' relationship with both the Father and the Son, reflecting the core theological understanding of the Godhead. This reminder of the believer's connection to the divine emphasizes the spiritual foundation upon which the ensuing discussions of relationships, forgiveness, and unity will be built.

4. Personal Connection: By addressing Philemon directly and invoking God's grace and peace upon him, Paul establishes a personal and relational context for the letter. This personal touch underscores Paul's genuine affection for Philemon and his desire to engage in a dialogue that goes beyond doctrinal teachings, delving into matters of the heart and Christian living.

In summary, Philemon 1:3 may appear as a simple greeting, but it encapsulates profound theological concepts and sets the stage for the transformative themes of the entire letter. The mention of grace and peace from God the Father and the Lord Jesus Christ lays the groundwork for discussions on forgiveness, reconciliation, and the transformative power of the gospel in the context of personal relationships. This verse serves as a reminder that the Christian journey is marked by the unmerited favor of God and the inner peace that comes from a relationship with Christ—a relationship that calls believers to extend grace and pursue peace in their interactions with one another.

Study and Discussion Guide Verse 3

1. What two blessings did Paul pray this Church would enjoy in verse   3?
a):
b):
2. What is the significance of the order in which these two blessings are named?
3. From whom did Paul say these blessings would flow in verse 3?
a):
b):
4. What person of the Trinity is not mentioned here?
5. What are some of the jobs and functions of the 3rd Person of the   Trinity?
a) John 16:8:
b) John 16:13:
c) Titus 3:5:

d) John 15:26; 16:14:
e) Acts 9:31:
f) Acts 20:28; 13:2:
g) Romans 8:14; Galatians 5:18; Matthew 4:1; Luke 4:1:
h) 2 Thessalonians 2:13; 1 Peter 1:2; Romans 5:16:
i) Acts 1:8, Luke 4:14; 24:49; Romans 15:19:
 j) Ephesians 5:18; Acts 2:4; 4:8, 31; 9:17:
k) Romans 8:26:
l) Matthew 12:28:
m) 2 Peter 1:21:
n) 1 Thessalonians 1:6:
o) Romans 8:16:
p) Galatians 5:22-23:
q) 1 Corinthians 12:1-11:
r) Ephesians 1:13; 4:3:
s) 1 Corinthians 2:11:

CHAPTER IV

Praying for You

Philemon 1:4 Expositor's Study:

Philemon 1:4 I thank my God, making mention of you always in my prayers,

Paul begins by acknowledging how Philemon's loving service and hospitality have refreshed him and other believers in Christ. Unconventionally, however, Paul prays for Philemon to grow in and spread his faith in Christ (vv4-7). This love, hospitality and faith will also provide the basis for Paul's appeal to Philemon for new action (v9). Paul's pastoral prayers of thanksgiving for the work of the gospel and the Holy Spirit in God's people were a regular feature at the beginning of his letters (cf. Romans 1:8; 1 Corinthians. 1:4; Ephesians 1:16; Philippians 1:3; Colossians 1:3; 1 Thessalonians 1:2).

In the world today, one of the best ways to manipulate another person into doing what you want is to tell people what they want to hear, and talk about how great they are. I would call this subtle emotional manipulation.

When Paul told Philemon that, "I thank my God, making mention of thee always in my prayers," he did not highlight Philemon. Three parts of this statement are of God. It was God he thanked, and to God he prayed. It was Philemon for whom he prayed. If we could remember to pray for those on our hearts as Paul did, we would not have time to scheme and manipulate others for our own purpose. It was God's purpose that held Paul's attention.

Paul is an example of a man that prayed often and earnestly for the saints – making mention of them always in His prayers and always giving thanks to God for the grace that had been bestowed on fellow believers. Paul demonstrated a deep desire for their spiritual growth and maturity - praying for opportunities for them to serve the Lord in the beauty of holiness.

These people had been such a blessing to Paul that Paul prayed for them often and with thanksgiving to God. We should remember to do the same for people who are a blessing in our own lives.

Paul was actually doing exactly what he preached. Paul tells us to pray in Ephesians 6:18 and 1 Timothy 2:1: Praying always with all prayer and supplication in the Spirit, and watching thereunto with all perseverance and supplication for all saints; Exhibit 1 Timothy 2:1 I exhort therefore, that, first of all, supplications, prayers, intercessions, and giving of thanks, be made for all men;

Following are Paul's example who followed Jesus' example, when we are impressed to pray for others. Here are some blessings we might pray for our friends that they enjoy.

"But the fruit of the Spirit is love, joy, peace, longsuffering, gentleness, goodness, faith, meekness, temperance" (Galatians 5:22-23)

In verses 4 through 7, as Paul set the stage for his request, he is being completely sincere in his compliments and praise.

Paul frequently used compliments and praise as a means to encourage and stimulate the people to whom he ministered. He was not a man to flatter people just to gain popularity. His words were sincere expressions of genuine appreciation. If they had done well, then Paul commended them - not in a way to puff them up, but in such a manner as to encourage them to continue in doing well.

Following Paul's example, there are many times when we can help people by a simple word of commendation. A sincere compliment is one of the best encouragements we can give.

In Verse 4, Apostle Paul's thanksgiving for Philemon was Godward, personal, and continual.: It was God he thanked, and to God he prayed. It was Philemon for whom he prayed. If we could remember to pray for those on our hearts as Paul did, we would not have time to scheme and manipulate others for our own purpose. It was God's purpose that held Paul's attention.

Pursuant to Colossians 4:12, Apostle Paul could have heard from Epaphras about what was going on with Philemon, when he himself was in Rome, in prison.

Epaphras was a distinguished disciple, and possibly the founder of the Colossian church. He was with Paul during part of his 1st Roman imprisonment, as we see in verse 23, where he is called by Paul his "fellow-prisoner." Paul's regard for him is shown by his designating him "our beloved fellow-servant," "a faithful minister of Christ" (Colossians 1:7), and "a bondservant of Christ Jesus" (Colossians 4:12).

Paul noticed the good things people did, and always remembered to thank them. Apostle Paul felt led to commend and thank the following Saints:
a) Romans 1:8-9: Saints in Rome
b) 1 Thessalonians 1:2-3: The church in Thessalonica
c) 1 Corinthians 1:4-6: The church of God which is at Corinth

We see that Paul not only thanked the people for what they were doing, but he also let them know that he always makes mention of them in his prayers.

These people had been such a blessing to Paul that Paul prayed for them often and with thanksgiving to God. We should remember to do the same for people who are a blessing in our own lives.

Paul was actually doing exactly what he preached. In Ephesians 6:18 and 1 Timothy 2:1, Paul is telling us to pray always with all prayer and supplication in the Spirit, and watching thereunto with all perseverance and supplication for all saints; Exhibit 1 Timothy 2:1 I exhort therefore, that, first of all, supplications, prayers, intercessions, and giving of thanks, be made for all men;

Following Paul's example who followed Jesus' example, when we are impressed to pray for others, the following are some blessings we might pray that they enjoy:

a) Ephesians 1:17: the spirit of wisdom and revelation in the knowledge of Him.

b) Ephesians 3:16: That he would grant you, according to the riches of his glory, to be strengthened with might by his Spirit in the inner man;

c) Ephesians 3:17: That Christ may dwell in our hearts by faith; that we, being rooted and grounded in love,

Paul prayed that they would KNOW the love of Christ. This is a spiritual reality, but Paul didn't want them to base their knowledge on feelings or emotions, but on the facts as revealed by the Holy Spirit.

d) Philippians 1:9: that our love may abound yet more and more in knowledge and in all judgment;

e) 1 Thessalonians 3:12: And the Lord make you to increase and abound in love one toward another, and toward all men, even as we do toward you

f) 1 Thessalonians 3:13: To the end he may stablish your hearts unblameable in holiness before God, even our Father, at the coming of our Lord Jesus Christ with all his saints.

g) 2 Thessalonians 1:11: Wherefore also we pray always for you, that our God would count you worthy of this calling, and fulfil all the good pleasure of his goodness, and the work of faith with power:

h) 2 Thessalonians 3:5: And the Lord direct your hearts into the love of God, and into the patient waiting for Christ.

Paul undoubtedly had felt God strengthen and protect him, and was confident that He would also help the Thessalonians as they were enduring persecution stirred up by the "evil one" in verse 3.

Philemon 1:4 Commentary:

The fourth verse of the Book of Philemon continues the introductory portion of the letter and provides insight into the apostle Paul's prayerful and thankful disposition toward Philemon. This verse reveals Paul's gratitude for Philemon's faith and love and sets the stage for the appeal and exhortations that follow.

"I thank my God always when I remember you in my prayers,"

In this verse, Paul begins by expressing his gratitude to God for Philemon. The phrase "I thank my God" conveys a sense of personal devotion and points to Paul's intimate relationship with God. The act of giving thanks indicates Paul's appreciation for Philemon and serves as a foundation for the forthcoming discussions within the letter.

"… always when I remember you in my prayers":

Paul's thankfulness is not just a casual sentiment; it is a regular, consistent practice. The phrase "always when I remember you in my prayers" emphasizes the intentional and ongoing nature of Paul's prayers for Philemon. This suggests that Philemon holds a special place in Paul's heart and that his thoughts of Philemon prompt him to approach God in prayer.

Key Themes and Implications:

1. Gratitude in Prayer: Paul's expression of gratitude within his prayers underscores the interconnectedness of his faith and his interactions with others. His prayer life is not confined to personal concerns but extends to those whom he cares about. This theme of gratitude models for believers the importance of intercessory prayer and the habit of regularly lifting up fellow believers before God.

2. Remembering and Relationship: The phrase "when I remember you in my prayers" signifies the depth of Paul's relationship with Philemon. The act of remembrance holds significance beyond mere recollection; it implies a deep

affection and a sense of shared experiences. Paul's remembrance of Philemon is tied to his prayers, indicating that their relationship is intertwined with their mutual commitment to the gospel.

3. Faith and Love: The fact that Paul's thanksgiving is specifically directed toward Philemon's faith and love highlights the foundational attributes of a Christian life. Faith reflects Philemon's trust in Christ, while love encompasses his compassion, kindness, and selflessness. These virtues are integral to the Christian identity and form the basis for the subsequent discussions on forgiveness and reconciliation.

4. Prayer as a Connection: Paul's practice of remembering Philemon in his prayers serves as a metaphorical thread that binds them together, even in physical separation. It conveys the idea that prayer creates a spiritual connection among believers, transcending distance and circumstances.

Personal Application:

Philemon 1:4 offers believers several points of personal application:

1. Intercessory Prayer: Paul's example encourages believers to engage in regular intercessory prayer for fellow believers. Praying for others demonstrates love, care, and solidarity within the body of Christ.

2. Gratitude for Faith and Love: Reflecting on the faith and love of fellow believers and expressing gratitude to God for them can deepen relationships and foster a sense of unity within the faith community.

3. Spiritual Connection: Recognizing the connection between prayer and relationships highlights the importance of maintaining spiritual bonds with fellow believers, even in times of physical separation.

4. Emphasis on Core Virtues: Paul's focus on faith and love reminds believers of the fundamental virtues that should characterize their lives and interactions with others.

In conclusion, Philemon 1:4 showcases Paul's heartfelt gratitude and consistent prayers for Philemon, reflecting the interconnectedness of faith, love, and prayer within the Christian community. This verse sets a tone of relational depth and spiritual concern that aligns with the themes of forgiveness, reconciliation, and Christian fellowship that are central to the remainder of the letter.

Study and Discussion Guide Verse 4

1. In the world today, one of the best ways to manipulate another person into doing what you want is to ...:
2. In verses 4 through 7, as Paul set the stage for his request, he is ...
3. Show how, in verse 4, Paul's thanksgiving for Philemon was Godward, personal, and continual
4. How could Paul have heard about what was going on with Philemon, when he himself was in Rome, in prison? (Colossians 4:12):
5. Paul noticed the good things people did, and always remembered to thank them. What had these saints done, that Paul felt led to commend and thank them?
a) Romans 1:8-9:
b) 1 Thessalonians 1:2-3:
c) 1 Corinthians 1:4-6:
6. In all four examples, we see that Paul not only thanked the people for what they were doing, but he also let them know that he always makes mention of them in his _____.:
7. Paul was actually doing exactly what he preached. For whom did Paul tell us to pray in Ephesians 6:18 and 1 Timothy 2:1?
 8. Following Paul's example who followed Jesus' example, when we are impressed to pray for others, what are some blessings we might pray that they enjoy?
a) Ephesians 1:17:
b) Ephesians 3:16:
c) Ephesians 3:17:
d) Philippians 1:9:
e) 1 Thessalonians 3:12:
f) 1 Thessalonians 3:13:

h) 2 Thessalonians 3:5:

CHAPTER V

The Attributes of Saints

Philemon 1:5 Expositor's Study:

Philemon 1:5 bearing of your love and faith which you have toward the Lord Jesus and toward all the saints,

In verse 5 there are two attributes of the saints been noticed by others in the community.

a): Love

b): Faith

Note: What others in the community see believers doing, and what they say about us is critical? It can make the different between a person accepting or rejecting Jesus Christ as their Lord and Savior. What qualities do unbelievers tend to notice, that could draw them toward the Lord, rather than away from Him?

a) Pursuant to 1 John 3:17: is to help a brother who is in need when we have the world's goods.

If you have the capability to meet a brother's needs, and do nothing to meet those needs, then how can you say you love that brother? John did not want believers to merely talk about love. He emphasized that real love is demonstrated in actions.

God calls us to be slow to anger. Don't let everything bother you to the point that you "lose it" or "blow up" every time someone makes a mistake. We all fail at times, even daily, and we will continue to do so until we reach heaven. Learn to interact with others using self-control, grace, and understanding.

b) 1 Timothy 6:6-8: To show godliness with contentment.

c) 1 Corinthians 1:10: To be in cohesion.

d) Matthew 25:21: To be good and faithful.

e) 1 Corinthians 9:27: To be disciplined and keep myself under control,

f) 1 Thessalonians 5:11: To encourage one another and build one another up,

g) Proverbs 16:11: To depend of the Lord: A just balance and scales are the Lord's; all the weights in the bag are his work.

h) Proverbs 14:29: To be slow in anger.

i) Luke 6:38: To share with others what we have. Give, and it will be given to you. Good measure, pressed down, shaken together, running over, will be put into your lap. For with the measure, you use it will be measured back to you."

j) Galatians 5:22-23: To show the fruit of the Spirit: love, joy, peace, patience, kindness, goodness, faithfulness, gentleness, self-control;

k) 1 Peter 3:10: To control your tongue. Exhibit: let him keep his tongue from evil and his lips from speaking deceit;

l) 1 Thessalonians 5:18: To give thanks in all circumstances.

m) Hebrews 13:18: To have a clear conscience, desiring to act honorably in all things.

n) Hebrews 13:2: To show hospitality to strangers.

Hospitality may be a lost art, but it is a command of God. In Old Testament times, travelers would arrive in the town square at the end of the day, knowing someone would invite them into their home. Jesus told His disciples to rely on the hospitality of others when He sent them out the first time.

Today, we tell people to come ANY time and stay with us, but we don't really mean it. After they arrive, we start to wonder when they're leaving. We are too busy with our ongoing schedules to make time for them. But if we begin to practice hospitality with an open heart instead of reluctance, it will lead to the community that God desires us to have, and it will lead others to Christ. We may even end up entertaining angels!

o) 1 Peter 5:5: To respect our elders: Exhibit: Likewise, you who are younger, be subject to the elders. Clothe yourselves, all of you, with humility toward one another, for "God opposes the proud but gives grace to the humble."

p) John 14:15: To love God and keep His commandments: Exhibit: If you love me, you will keep my commandments.

q) Hebrews 10:36: To show endurance. Exhibit: For you have need of endurance, so that when you have done the will of God you may receive what is promised.

r) Galatians 6:9: To never get tired of doing good. Exhibit: And let us not grow weary of doing good, for in due season we will reap, if we do not give up.

Below are few things we do, sometimes by habit or without even thinking, that might cause an unbeliever to turn away from the truth.:

a): Cheating in taxes

b): Telling lies

c): Cursing

d): Gossiping

Gossip always betrays a confidence (Proverbs 11;13). Most of us have been betrayed by a person with whom we have shared something in confidence. For the unbeliever, this can cause him/her to reject not only the gossiping person, but also the Person of Jesus Christ.

All these things can easily become habits, and offend others without our even thinking twice about them.

There are some specific things that God has said that He hates. If we do these things, we will not only offend God, but we can become a stumbling block for others. What are they? (Proverbs 6:17-19):

a): haughty eyes,

b): a lying tongue,

c): hands that shed innocent blood,

d): a heart that devises wicked plans

e): feet that make haste to run to evil,

f): a false witness who breathes out lies,

g): one who sows discord among brothers.

About what did the Apostle Paul warn the Corinthians in 1 Corinthians 8:9?

Self-righteous: Exhibit: But take care that this right of yours does not somehow become a stumbling block to the weak.

The prevailing attitude today is, "What I do is my own business." Most people believe they are not responsible to anyone else, and no one else has the right to make demands or claims on us with regard to their behavior.

Don't accept this way of thinking. We do not live-in isolation. Jesus did free his followers from the burden of the law, but this freedom carries responsibility. Jesus said we will have to answer to Him if we cause someone else to sin. We must not fail to recognize that the things we do will influence and have an impact upon others' lives.

Philemon 1:5 Commentary:

The fifth verse of the Book of Philemon provides a glimpse into the apostle Paul's appreciation for Philemon's involvement in the faith community and his acts of love toward fellow believers. This verse serves as a bridge between Paul's expressions of gratitude and the specific request he will make to Philemon regarding Onesimus.

"because I hear of your love and of the faith that you have toward the Lord Jesus and for all the saints,"

In this verse, Paul articulates his reasons for being thankful and encouraged by Philemon's character and actions:

"because I hear of your love and of the faith that you have toward the Lord Jesus": Paul commends Philemon's love and faith, highlighting his devotion to Christ. Love and faith are foundational virtues of the Christian life, and Philemon's demonstrated commitment to both Christ and his teachings is worthy of praise. This emphasis on faith points to Philemon's trust in the Lord Jesus, while the emphasis on love underscores his genuine care for others.

"and for all the saints": Philemon's love and faith are not limited to his personal relationship with Christ; they extend to his interactions with "all the saints." This demonstrates Philemon's active participation in the broader Christian community and his willingness to care for and support fellow believers. The term "saints" refers to all those who have been set apart and dedicated to God, signifying the entire body of believers.

Key Themes and Implications:

1. Christian Virtues: The combination of love and faith serves as a testament to Philemon's character as a believer. Love, characterized by selflessness and compassion, aligns with Christ's teachings and exemplifies the commandment to love one's neighbor as oneself. Faith, on the other hand, signifies Philemon's trust in God's promises and his commitment to the Lordship of Jesus Christ.

2. Community and Fellowship: The phrase "for all the saints" emphasizes Philemon's engagement in the Christian community. It underscores the importance of mutual support, fellowship, and a shared sense of belonging among believers. Philemon's love extends beyond mere sentiment to practical care and consideration for the well-being of his fellow brothers and sisters in Christ.

3. Inspiration and Encouragement: Paul's awareness of Philemon's love and faith serves to encourage both Philemon and the broader Christian audience. It highlights the impact that individual actions of love and faith can have on the larger community, inspiring others to emulate such virtues.

4. Unity in Diversity: The commendation of Philemon's love for "all the saints" reflects the diverse nature of the early Christian community. It suggests that love and faith

transcend cultural, social, and geographical boundaries, uniting believers in a common bond of devotion to Christ.

Personal Application:

Philemon 1:5 offers several points of personal application for believers:

1. Exemplifying Love and Faith: Believers are called to emulate Philemon's example by cultivating a deep love for Christ and actively demonstrating that love through acts of kindness, compassion, and care for fellow believers.

2. Engagement in Community: Like Philemon, believers are encouraged to actively participate in their local faith communities, showing love and support for "all the saints."

3. Encouragement through Testimony: Sharing stories of love and faith within the faith community can inspire and uplift others, fostering a sense of unity and shared purpose.

4. Recognizing God's Work: Observing and acknowledging the love and faith of fellow believers can serve as a reminder of God's transformative work in the lives of His people.

In conclusion, Philemon 1:5 sheds light on Philemon's commendable character and actions, emphasizing his love and faith toward the Lord Jesus and his fellow saints. This verse reinforces the significance of love and faith within the Christian journey and highlights the interconnectedness of believers within the larger body of Christ. Paul's appreciation for Philemon's virtues sets the stage for the sensitive request he will soon make regarding Onesimus, presenting a compelling case for reconciliation and unity within the context of Christian relationships.

Study and Discussion Guide Verse 5

1. For what two attributes had these saints been noticed by others in the community? (vs. 5):

a):

b):

2. What others in the community see believers doing, and what

they say about us is critical. It can make the different between a person accepting or rejecting Jesus Christ as their Lord and Savior. What qualities do unbelievers tend to notice, that could draw them toward the Lord, rather than away from Him?
a) 1 John 3:17:
b) 1 Timothy 6:6-8:
c) 1 Corinthians 1:10:
d) Matthew 25:21:
e) 1 Corinthians 9:27:
f) 1 Thessalonians 5:11:
g) Proverbs 16:11:
h) Proverbs 14:29:
i) Luke 6:38:
j) Galatians 5:22-23:
k) 1 Peter 3:10:
l) 1 Thessalonians 5:18:
m) Hebrews 13:18:
n) Hebrews 13:2:
o) 1 Peter 5:5:
p) John 14:15:
q) Hebrews 10:36:
r) Galatians 6:9:
3. List a few things we do, sometimes by habit or without even thinking, that might cause an unbeliever to turn away from the truth.:
a):
b):
c):
4. There are some specific things that God has said that He hates. If we do these things, we will not only offend God, but we can become a stumbling block for others. What are they? (Proverbs 6:17-19):

CHAPTER VI

Verse 6-7 Paul is Praying for Philemon

Philemon 1:6-7 Expositor's Study:

Philemon 6-7 that the sharing of your faith may become effective by the acknowledgment of every good thing which is in you in Christ Jesus. ⁷ For we have great joy and consolation in your love, because the hearts of the saints have been refreshed by you, brother.

In verses 6 and 7, Paul is praying for Philemon to shared his faith.

a): the communication of Philemon faith may become effectual by the acknowledging of every good thing which is in you in Christ Jesus.

b): the bowels of the saints are refreshed

These are all things that will be present when evangelism is effective. Your witness will become the overflow of a life touched and changed by God.

We can see Apostle Paul is acknowledging of every good thing which is in you in Christ Jesus which was the key to making an effective sharing of your faith, and this is why some are not effective in sharing their faith. They don't know or can't communicate properly every good thing God has done for us.

What does Paul encourage us to do in Ephesians 4:1?

To walk worthy of the vocation wherewith we are called.

c) What Bible verse is your "go-to verse" when problems start accelerating in your life?

Romans 4: 20 He staggered not at the promise of God through unbelief; but was strong in faith, giving glory to God; 21 And being fully persuaded that, what he had promised, he was able also to perform.

d) Saying you're a Christian is one thing, but living it in tangible ways every day is something else. Matthew 7:16 says, ": Ye shall know them by their fruits. Do men gather grapes of thorns, or figs of thistles?

e) Don't compromise your beliefs. Proverbs 10:9 warns us that we might get away with things for a while, but eventually his ways shall be known.

f) Become a model of forgiveness. According to Paul's letter to the Ephesians, we should not only forgive one another, but also ... (Ephesians 4:32): be ye kind one to another and tenderhearted,

g) And finally, don't forget to spend time in the Word, so when you have the chance to share your faith, you are ready. Paul told Timothy in 2 Timothy 2:15: Study to shew thyself approved unto God, a workman that needeth not to be ashamed, rightly dividing the word of truth.

This analogy may have come to Paul's mind because he was a tentmaker by profession (Acts 18:3). He knew there was a right way and a wrong way to cut the cloth, so there wouldn't be any waste.

The point is clear: There is a right way and a wrong way to divide the Word. We must continue to study and prepare, so we are able to answer questions accurately, and present the Gospel correctly.

4. What had given Paul great joy and comfort, even though he was imprisoned? (vs. 7): The love of Philemon

In addition, he had seen how Philemon's love spilled over to other brothers in Christ, evidenced by his works of charity toward them.

5. At the end of verse 7, what term did Paul use to re-emphasize his close feelings for Philemon? He called him Brother

Philemon 1:6-7 Commentary:

Verses 6 and 7 of the Book of Philemon reveal Paul's heartfelt prayer for Philemon and his expression of joy over the way Philemon's love and faith have blessed the community of believers.

6 I pray that the sharing of your faith may become effective for the full knowledge of every good thing that is in us for the sake of Christ. 7 For I have derived much joy and comfort from your love, my brother, because the hearts of the saints have been refreshed through you.

Verse 6: "I pray that the sharing of your faith may become effective for the full knowledge of every good thing that is in us for the sake of Christ."

In these verses, Paul shifts from offering gratitude to engaging in intercessory prayer on Philemon's behalf. His prayer is multi-dimensional:

- Sharing of Faith: Paul prays for Philemon's "sharing of faith" to become effective. This implies that Philemon's faith is not just a personal matter but something meant to be shared and lived out in community. It's a call to active Christian witness and service.

- Full Knowledge: Paul desires this sharing of faith to lead to "the full knowledge of every good thing." This refers to a deepening and comprehensive understanding of the blessings, virtues, and truths that accompany the Christian life.

- • For the Sake of Christ: The purpose of this sharing and knowledge is "for the sake of Christ." It underscores the centrality of Christ in all aspects of the believer's life and the motivation to bring honor and glory to Him.

Verse 7: "For I have derived much joy and comfort from your love, my brother, because the hearts of the saints have been refreshed through you."

- • Joy and Comfort: Paul expresses his personal joy and comfort derived from Philemon's love. This love is not only a source of happiness but also provides encouragement and solace to Paul, emphasizing the close bond they share as brothers in Christ.
- • Refreshment of Hearts: Paul acknowledges that the love demonstrated by Philemon has a positive impact on the hearts of fellow believers. Philemon's actions have a refreshing effect, contributing to the spiritual well-being and renewal of the community of saints.

Key Themes and Implications:

1. Effective Sharing of Faith: These verses underscore the significance of actively sharing one's faith. The Christian faith is not meant to be private; it should be shared in a way that promotes the growth and understanding of others.
2. Comprehensive Knowledge: The desire for "full knowledge of every good thing" emphasizes the ongoing process of spiritual growth and learning. It reflects the idea that the Christian journey involves continuous discovery and understanding of the blessings and truths of Christ.
3. Impact of Love: Philemon's love has far-reaching effects. His actions not only bring joy to individuals like Paul but also refresh and uplift the entire community of believers. This highlights the communal aspect of the Christian faith.
4. Christ-Centered Living: The central purpose of sharing faith and growing in knowledge is "for the sake of Christ." This reminds believers that all their efforts and actions

should ultimately reflect Christ's influence and bring glory to Him.

Personal Application:

1. Active Witness: Believers are encouraged to actively share their faith through both words and deeds, aiming to have a positive impact on others' understanding of Christ and His teachings.

2. Lifelong Learning: The pursuit of "full knowledge" should be a continuous endeavor, prompting believers to seek deeper understanding of God's Word and its application in their lives.

3. Impactful Love: Acts of love have the power to refresh and uplift the hearts of fellow believers. Demonstrating love not only strengthens relationships but also contributes to the spiritual well-being of the community.

4. Christ-Centered Motivation: All efforts, whether in sharing faith or demonstrating love, should be grounded in a desire to honor Christ and further His kingdom.

In conclusion, Philemon 1:6-7 highlights the importance of active sharing of faith, continuous spiritual growth, and the transformative impact of love within the Christian community. These verses remind believers of their responsibility to contribute positively to the spiritual well-being of others and emphasize the centrality of Christ in all aspects of their lives. The themes of community, love, and Christ-centered living laid out in these verses provide a solid foundation for the subsequent appeal Paul makes to Philemon regarding the matter of Onesimus.

Study and Discussion Guide Verse 6-7:

1. In verses 6 and 7, what did Paul pray would be the result when Philemon shared his faith?

a):

b):

2. What did Paul say was the key to making an effective sharing of your faith?

3. God designed an easy evangelism program. He made it simple for   us,:

a) Briefly summarize your own story here.:

b) What does Paul encourage us to do in Ephesians 4:1?

c) What Bible verse is your "go-to verse" when problems start accelerating in your life?

d) Saying you're a Christian is one thing, but living it in tangible ways every day is something else. Matthew 7:16 says, ":

e) Don't compromise your beliefs. Proverbs 10:9 warns us that we might get away with things for a while, but eventually …:

f) Become a model of forgiveness. According to Paul's letter to the Ephesians, we should not only forgive one another, but also... (Ephesians 4:32):

g) And finally, don't forget to spend time in the Word, so when you have the chance to share your faith, you are ready. Paul told Timothy in 2 Timothy 2:15:

4. What had given Paul great joy and comfort, even though he was imprisoned? (vs. 7):

5. At the end of verse 7, what term did Paul use to re-emphasize his close feelings for Philemon?

CHAPTER VII

The Plea for Onesimus

Philemon 1:8-9 Expositor's Study:

Philemon 8-9 8 Therefore, though I might be very bold in Christ to command you what is fitting, 9 yet for love's sake I rather appeal to you—being such a one as Paul, the aged, and now also a prisoner of Jesus Christ—

The Plea for Onesimus:

In verse 8, Paul said that it would have much easier, more convenient, to simply command that Philemon to the thing he was about to ask. Paul wasn't hesitant to command when the situation demanded it. For example, in 1 Corinthians 5:4-5, what did Paul command that the believers do in the case of the church member fornicating with his father's wife? To deliver such one unto Satan for the destruction of the flesh

Paul's command also served the important purpose of removing any false feeling of security the sinning man might have among the fellowship of Christians. They couldn't just ignore his sin, and let him ignore it, pretending it wasn't there. If the man refused to face his sin, the church must face it for him, for his sake and for their sake.

Shunning still occurs in Old Order Amish and some Mennonite churches today, and is particularly painful for those in congregations where the people are very close-knit. However, I don't think this would work in most churches today. Often people leave their church and "try out" another without a second thought. And mega-churches have gotten so large, we never enjoy that close connection with others where shunning could make an impact.

However, in wisdom Paul knew when to use another approach. In verse 9, Paul highlighted that he was writing this request for love's sake.

Paul appealed for love's sake instead of wording this as a command. However, Paul made it clear that he had the right to command what was fitting - yet he still appealed in love.

Looking ahead, what situation was unfolding where Philemon might find it difficult to respond with love, unless he did so with the love with which he was redeemed by the blood of Jesus? Find forgiveness in his heart for Onesimus, his former servant.

When Paul made this appeal on behalf of Onesimus, he was following deep traditions in Roman culture. There was an ancient Greek law (inherited by the Romans) allowing any escaped slave sanctuary at an altar. The altar could even be the hearth of a private family home. Then the head of the family was obligated to give the slave protection while he tried to persuade him to return to his master. If the slave refused, the head of the family would put the slave up for auction and give the price for the slave to the former master.

Paul gave Onesimus protection, and now was working the issue out with Philemon.

In this verse, Paul appealed to Philemon's sympathies by the way he described himself and his circumstances. What were the two points he made about himself as an intercessor?

a): the aged

b): and a prisoner

Before asking the favor, Paul appealed to Philemon's sympathies by highlighting his own challenges.

In the King James Version, Paul refers to himself as being aged, and in other versions, this is translated "an old man." Commentators believe Paul was about 56+ at the time of this epistle, based on his age at the time of Stephen's stoning. What does Acts 7:58 say about his age at the time of the stoning? a young man

The older (aged), more mature men in these new churches often served as bishops and deacons. What are some qualifications Paul required of older men who wanted to serve in the church?

a) Titus 2:2: That the aged men be sober, grave, temperate, sound in faith, in charity, in patience.

b) 1 Timothy 3:12: Let the deacons be the husbands of one wife, ruling their children and their own houses well.

In Titus 2:3, Paul listed several things women should do, as they age? What are they?

a): be in behavior as becometh holiness,

b): not false accusers,

c): not given to much wine,

d): teachers of good things;

However, their advice may have been more readily accepted by the young women in that day. Sadly, today, young women often (usually?) reject the advice of older women.

Here are some things the elderly, both men and women, can and should be teaching:

- Declare the Lord is upright; He is our rock, and there is no unrighteousness in Him (Psalm 92:15).
- Proclaim God's strength to the next generation (Psalm 71:17-18).
- Recount God's mighty works to the next generation (Psalm 78:1-8).

a) The current thinking among many older people is that they have already put in their time to serve. They believe it is time for the younger people to step up to the plate, and do the work of the church. They believe when they retire from their workplace jobs, it is also time to retire from their church jobs. Would you agree with this?
b) If you don't agree, list some areas in which an elderly person's assistance or input could be used.:
c) To help in reconciliation
d) To teach and give word of wisdom
e) Praying for those who are in need

Didn't God design the local church to be overseen by elders? We always think of this term as the title for a position, and have forgotten that originally this position was to be given to men who were older, elderly, capable of teaching and leading the flock (Acts 14:23; Titus 1:5-9) and men who could serve as overseers and examples (1Peter 5:1-4).

Name two Old Testament heroes who were called to serve God at a time in their lives when we would probably say they were "past their prime.:

a): Elijah
b): Elisha

And here's a few more possible answers.

- Joshua was given the charge of leading the conquest of Canaan, during the last thirty years of his life. He lived until he was 110 (Joshua 24:29), so he was 80 when Moses left him in charge.

- Caleb was also very much involved in the conquest of Canaan, and he was in his eighties (Joshua 14:6-11).

- Zacharias and Elizabeth were the parents of John the Baptist, and they were both well advanced in years (Luke 1:7).

- Simeon and Anna were two elderly people who bore witness to the Christ child when He was presented to the temple to be circumcised (Luke 2:25-38). Anna herself was at least 84, and had been serving God "with fasting and prayers night and day."

The word used for "aged" in this verse could also be translated "ambassador," which may be the meaning Paul actually intended. The Amplified and Good News Bibles use this translation instead.:

a) What is an ambassador? one who is sent to represent one country or government to another.

b) For whom was the Apostle Paul an ambassador? Ambassador for Jesus Christ.

c) According to 2 Corinthians 5:20, who should be ambassadors? We are ambassadors for Christ

d) Just as Paul followed the example of Jesus, and encouraged us to follow his own example, we should all watch such worthy mentors and follow their example.

Philemon 1:8-9 Commentary:

Verses 8 and 9 of the Book of Philemon mark a turning point in the letter, as the apostle Paul begins to address a specific request concerning Onesimus, Philemon's runaway slave. Paul's approach is characterized by both humility and authority as he appeals to Philemon's sense of love, respect, and obligation.

"8 Accordingly, though I am bold enough in Christ to command you to do what is required, 9 yet for love's sake I prefer to appeal to you—I, Paul, an old man and now a prisoner also for Christ Jesus—"

Verse 8: "Accordingly, though I am bold enough in Christ to command you to do what is required…"

In this verse, Paul acknowledges his authority in Christ, which grants him the ability to issue commands. However, he tempers this authority with sensitivity to the relationship he shares with Philemon and the context of their faith.

- Boldness in Christ: Paul acknowledges that he has the authority to issue commands as an apostle and servant of Christ. His confidence stems from his position as a representative of Christ's teachings.
- What Is Required: The phrase "to command you to do what is required" indicates that Paul could impose his authority

to demand a certain course of action. This phrase sets the stage for the matter he is about to address concerning Onesimus.

Verse 9: "yet for love's sake I prefer to appeal to you…"

Paul immediately follows his acknowledgment of authority with an expression of his preferred approach—a gentle and heartfelt appeal.

- For Love's Sake: Paul's appeal is motivated by love, emphasizing the relational and compassionate aspect of his request. He wishes to approach Philemon with a spirit of mutual understanding and respect.
- Appeal: Paul's decision to appeal rather than command demonstrates his desire to foster a response rooted in Philemon's willingness and free choice. He seeks a response motivated by genuine conviction rather than mere obligation.

"…I, Paul, an old man and now a prisoner also for Christ Jesus—"

- Identification: Paul emphasizes his personal connection to the situation. He refers to himself as "an old man," potentially appealing to Philemon's sense of honor and respect. Additionally, he mentions his current status as a prisoner for Christ, which may evoke empathy and solidarity.

Key Themes and Implications:

1. Authority and Humility: Paul's acknowledgment of his authority contrasts with his humility and preference for a gentler approach. This combination reflects the balance between leadership and humility that characterizes effective Christian leadership.
2. Love and Relationship: Paul's appeal is rooted in love and mutual relationship. This theme underscores the importance of approaching difficult conversations with empathy, compassion, and a focus on maintaining healthy connections.
3. Free Will and Choice: The decision to appeal rather than command highlights the principle of free will within Christian relationships. It reinforces the idea that true

obedience and cooperation arise from a genuine heart response.

4. Shared Experience: Paul's mention of his own circumstances, as an old man and a prisoner, creates a sense of shared experience. This potentially fosters a sense of camaraderie and encourages Philemon to relate to Paul's perspective.

Personal Application:

1. Balancing Authority and Sensitivity: Leaders within the church and in personal relationships can learn from Paul's approach, blending authority with sensitivity and empathy.

2. Appealing through Love: When addressing challenging matters, appealing through love and understanding can lead to more meaningful and lasting resolutions.

3. Respect for Free Will: Recognizing and respecting the free will of others promotes a culture of mutual respect and genuine engagement in decisions.

4. Sharing Experiences: Sharing personal experiences can create relatability and understanding, fostering a deeper connection within Christian communities.

In conclusion, Philemon 1:8-9 showcases Paul's tactful and heartfelt approach to addressing a delicate matter with Philemon. The interplay between authority, love, and humility reflects the principles of effective communication, mutual respect, and the importance of maintaining healthy relationships within the body of Christ. Paul's appeal sets the stage for the subsequent request concerning Onesimus, illustrating how Christian principles can guide even the most challenging conversations.

Study and Discussion Guide Verse 8-9:

1. In verse 8, Paul said that it would have much easier, more convenient, to simply command that Philemon to the thing he was about to ask. Paul wasn't hesitant to command when the situation demanded it. For example, in 1 Corinthians 5:4-5, what did Paul command that the believers do in the case of the church member fornicating with his father's wife?

2. However, in wisdom Paul knew when to use another approach. In verse 9, Paul highlighted that he was writing this request for _______ sake.:

3. Looking ahead, what situation was unfolding where Philemon might find it difficult to respond with love, unless he did so with the love with which he was redeemed by the blood of Jesus?

4. In this verse, Paul appealed to Philemon's sympathies by the way he described himself and his circumstances. What were the two points he made about himself as an intercessor?

a):

b):

5. In the King James Version, Paul refers to himself as being aged, and in other versions, this is translated "an old man." Commentators believe Paul was about 56+ at the time of this epistle, based on his age at the time of Stephen's stoning. What does Acts 7:58 say about his age at the time of the stoning? a young man

6. The older (aged), more mature men in these new churches often served as bishops and deacons. What are some qualifications Paul required of older men who wanted to serve in the church?

a) Titus 2:2:

b) 1 Timothy 3:12:

 7. In Titus 2:3, Paul listed several things women should do, as they age? What are they?

a):

b):

c):

d):

8. a) The current thinking among many older people is that they have already put in their time to serve. They believe it is time for the younger people to step up to the plate, and do the work of the church. They believe when they retire from their workplace jobs, it is also time to retire from their church jobs. Would you agree with this?

If you don't agree, list some areas in which an elderly person's assistance or input could be used.:

b):

c):

d):

9. Name two Old Testament heroes who were called to serve God at a time in their lives when we would probably say they were "past their prime.:

a):

b):

10. The word used for "aged" in this verse could also be translated "ambassador," which may be the meaning Paul actually intended. The Amplified and Good News Bibles use this translation instead.:

a) What is an ambassador?

b) For whom was the Apostle Paul an ambassador?

c) According to 2 Corinthians 5:20, who should be ambassadors?

d) Name a person who is either well-known, or someone you know personally, who serves as an on-fire ambassador for Christ, and tell a little about their story.:

CHAPTER VIII

An Appeal to Philemon

Philemon 1:10 Expositor's Study:

Philemon 1:10 I appeal to you for my son Onesimus, whom I have begotten while in my chains,

This is an identifier for Philemon, as Paul puts him in the same family! Onesimus had wronged Philemon, and had run away. When he came to Rome, he heard that Paul was in prison, and came to see him. It was there that Paul led him to a saving knowledge of the Lord Jesus, Y'shua Moshiach. Onesimus became a believer.

The relationship Paul claimed between himself and Onesimus in verse 10 is of the Father and Son.

What had happened that led Paul to say that Onesimus was now a member of his own family? Onesimus did something bad to Philemon, in contrast, Apostle Paul is giving Philemon the news that he must find forgiveness in his heart for Onesimus, his former servant.

Accordingly, in this verse shows that Paul had ministered to Onesimus and spent quality time with him. He could honestly describe his character. It confirms Paul had explained the scriptures to him and seen Onesimus accept the good news of the gospel and salvation by grace through faith.

In addition, we can be sure that the relationship didn't stop after Onesimus left the prison. It didn't with Titus, or Timothy, or the churches that Paul started. Paul was a true friend who stuck by his "children" of the faith for life.

This was a difficult situation all around.:

a) It would be difficult for Philemon to take Onesimus back because Onesimus had wronged Philemon, and had run away.

I think pride could have gotten in the way of this request. Philemon was a slaveowner. And he would have been raised from childhood to take pride in his wealth and status. In addition, this runaway slave had stolen from him to finance the escape. Up to this point, Philemon probably thought of Onesimus as a dirt bag, a worthless scoundrel who deserved whatever he got.

But Paul was asking Philemon to forgive and forget. Total and absolute forgiveness takes years of practice in humility, compassion, sympathy, understanding, tolerance and sensitivity to fellow beings. We will never acquire these virtues until we start melting our ego.

b) It would be difficult for Onesimus to carry Paul's letter to Philemon because he was a slave who had run away and we do not know the full scope of injury that he imposed on Philemon,

c) And, from a selfish standpoint, it was going to be difficult for Paul to send Onesimus back to Colossae because ... (vs. 13).: Whom I would have retained with me, that in thy stead he might have ministered unto me in the bonds of the gospel:

Paul was sharing friendship in one of the truest ways friendships can be shown. Paul was writing a letter of recommendation to Philemon. Paul was putting his reputation on the line to stand up for Onesimus. It's always good to have friends you can count on - not only to give us a good letter of recommendation when we need one, but to help us through life itself.

In those days, a master had the legal right to kill a runaway slave, but Paul was asking Philemon to not only forgive Onesimus, but also to accept Onesimus as a brother in Christ.

Because God is willing to wipe our slates clean and accept us as His sons and daughters, we should always be willing to ... (Matthew 6:12).: forgive our debtors.

Everybody is precious in God's sight. And it is important that we recognize that no matter what we have done we can have a fresh start in Christ. As Onesimus got a fresh start with Philemon, we should also be willing to give people a second chance.

The Apostle Paul addressed the issue of forgiveness in Ephesians 4:31-32, when he said that we should:

a) vs. 31: Let all bitterness, and wrath, and anger, and clamour, and evil speaking, be put away from you, with all malice:

b) vs. 32: And be ye kind one to another, tenderhearted, forgiving one another, even as God for Christ's sake hath forgiven you.

Do you know who is Tychicus?

Final Greetings

Colossians 4:7-9 [7] Tychicus, a beloved brother, faithful minister, and fellow servant in the Lord, will tell you all the news about me. [8] I am sending him to you for this very purpose, that [a] he may know your circumstances and comfort your hearts, [9] with Onesimus, a faithful and beloved brother, who is one of you. They will make known to you all things which are happening here.

Who would be going back with Onesimus, and carrying a separate letter to the Colossians? (Colossians 4:7-9):

Tychicus was a behind the scenes kind of guy, out of sight, and out of mind type of Christian servant.

- It's not that he wasn't active - he was.
- It's not that he wasn't known or appreciated - he was.

- It's not that he felt alone and not needed - he was surrounded by friends and knew he was needed.

Acts 20:4 And Sopater of Berea accompanied him to Asia— also Aristarchus and Secundus of the Thessalonians, and Gaius of Derbe, and Timothy, and Tychicus and Trophimus of Asia.

What can we learn about this person from Acts 20:4? He was one of Paul's companions. We can also learn some important qualities about Tychicus' character.

- He was selfless (beloved brother - Colossians 4:7).
- He was steadfast (faithful minister - Colossians 4:7)
- He was sensitive (that he might comfort your hearts - Colossians 4:8)

What was the other church to which this same person also carried a letter? (Ephesians 6:21-22): Ephesus

Ephesians 6:21-22

New King James Version

A Gracious Greeting

21 But that you also may know my affairs and how I am doing, Tychicus, a beloved brother and faithful minister in the Lord, will make all things known to you; 22 whom I have sent to you for this very purpose, that you may know our affairs, and that he may comfort your hearts.

Onesimus would have run again or maybe even kill himself because of fear or he might have never returned to Philemon and gone somewhere else. Notice that Paul didn't call Tychicus a friend, but a brother. Proverbs 17.17 says that a friend loves at all times, and a brother is born for adversity. This was a sticky situation where there was definitely the potential for adversity when Onesimus came face-to-face with Philemon for the first time. The situation could have gone south quickly.

Brothers and sisters in Christ have been placed in our lives for times of adversity. When situations threaten to overwhelm us, most of us still have members of our blood families. But sometimes they don't know how to pray with us, how to give godly advice. When we need someone to stand with us in faith, we need our brothers and sisters in Christ. If our own family members are also our brothers and sisters in Christ, we are blessed.

If Onesimus were going back on his own, alone with his private thoughts and fears, what might have been the final result?

Philemon 1:10 Commentary:

"I appeal to you for my child, Onesimus, whose father I became in my imprisonment."

In this verse, the apostle Paul introduces the central focus of his letter to Philemon—the plea for Onesimus, Philemon's runaway slave. Paul's choice of words underscores his personal connection to Onesimus and the transformative power of the gospel.

"I appeal to you:" The tone of Paul's appeal remains gentle and relational, emphasizing his desire for Philemon's understanding and cooperation rather than a forceful demand. This approach aligns with the themes of love, forgiveness, and unity that Paul intends to highlight.

"for my child, Onesimus:" The use of the term "my child" reveals the deep spiritual relationship that has developed between Paul and Onesimus. Through his ministry, Paul has acted as a spiritual father to Onesimus, highlighting the transformative impact of the gospel in bringing about new identities and relationships.

"whose father I became in my imprisonment:" Paul's mention of his imprisonment draws attention to the circumstances under which he and Onesimus came to know each other. Despite the challenging context, Paul's imprisonment becomes a backdrop for God's redemptive work, as he describes himself as a spiritual father to Onesimus. This imagery of a new family dynamic contrasts with the slave-master relationship that previously existed between Onesimus and Philemon.

Relevant Bible Verses:

1. Galatians 4:19 (ESV): "My little children, for whom I am again in the anguish of childbirth until Christ is formed in you!" - This verse from Galatians demonstrates Paul's use of familial language and the concept of spiritual birth.

2. 1 Corinthians 4:15 (ESV): "For though you have countless guides in Christ, you do not have many fathers. For I became your father in Christ Jesus through the gospel." - Paul's role as a spiritual father is highlighted here, emphasizing the impact of the gospel in forming new relationships.

3. 1 Timothy 1:2 (ESV): "To Timothy, my true child in the faith: Grace, mercy, and peace from God the Father and Christ Jesus our Lord." - Similar to his relationship with Onesimus, Paul refers to Timothy as his spiritual child in the faith.

Key Themes and Implications:

1. Transformative Power of the Gospel: The mention of Onesimus as Paul's "child" speaks to the transformative power of the gospel in reshaping identities and relationships. Paul's relationship with Onesimus illustrates the radical changes that occur when individuals encounter Christ.

2. Redemption and Reconciliation: Paul's reference to becoming a father to Onesimus in his imprisonment highlights the redemptive and reconciling work of Christ. It suggests that even in the midst of challenging circumstances, God can bring about new beginnings and healing.

3. Familial Language: Paul's use of familial language (father and child) emphasizes the sense of spiritual kinship and unity that believers share in Christ. This language underscores the interconnectedness of the Christian community.

4. Context of Imprisonment: The mention of Paul's imprisonment serves as a reminder that the gospel message is not confined by physical limitations. Even in times of hardship, God's transformative work continues to shape lives and relationships.

Personal Application:

1. Forgiveness and Reconciliation: Paul's relationship with Onesimus illustrates the potential for forgiveness and reconciliation, even in complex and challenging situations.
2. Spiritual Family: Believers can find solace and support within the larger spiritual family, where relationships are grounded in faith and shared commitment to Christ.
3. New Identities in Christ: Just as Onesimus experienced a new identity as a child of Paul through the gospel, believers are reminded of their identity as children of God through faith in Christ.
4. Impact of Ministry: Paul's example highlights the transformative impact of ministry and mentorship, demonstrating the potential to influence lives and shape spiritual growth.

In conclusion, Philemon 1:10 introduces the theme of transformation and redemption through Paul's appeal for Onesimus, whom he regards as a spiritual child. The verse highlights the familial language used to describe relationships within the faith community and underscores the power of the gospel to reshape identities and bring about reconciliation. Paul's plea for Onesimus sets the stage for the subsequent request he makes to Philemon, inviting him to extend forgiveness and grace to his former slave.

Study and Discussion Guide Verse 10:

1.What relationship did Paul claim between himself and Onesimus in verse 10?2. What had happened that led Paul to say that Onesimus was now a member of his own family?

3. This was a difficult situation all around.:

a) It would be difficult for Philemon to take Onesimus back because ...:

b) It would be difficult for Onesimus to carry Paul's letter to Philemon because ...:

c) And, from a selfish standpoint, it was going to be difficult for Paul to send Onesimus back to Colossae because ... (vs. 13).:

4. In those days, a master had the legal right to kill a runaway slave, but Paul was asking Philemon to not only forgive Onesimus, but also to accept Onesimus as a brother in _______.:

5. Because God is willing to wipe our slates clean and accept us as His sons and daughters, we should always be willing to ... (Matthew 6:12).:

CHAPTER IX

Unprofitable to Profitable

Philemon 1:11-12 Expositor's Study:

Philemon 1:11-12, 11 who once was unprofitable to you, but now is profitable to you and to me. 12 I am sending him back. You therefore receive him, that is, my own heart,

How had becoming a Christian changed Onesimus? (vs. 11):

Onesimus is now a believer and profitable to all. Which in time past was to thee unprofitable, but now profitable to thee and to me. Paul pulls no punches in hitting Philemon with hard facts. He knew the story, and what had happened. He knew the problem, since Onesimus was a slave who had run away. We do not know the full scope of injury that he imposed on Philemon, but it was substantial for Paul to be sending such a plea.

I was just wondering ... did Onesimus run away to avoid getting caught after he stole something? Or did he steal something so he would have the money to eat when he ran away? I had assumed one thing, but it could have been the other way around. The Scripture doesn't actually say.

HOWEVER, the Scripture is clear about this. Onesimus was now a changed man, a new creation in Christ.

2. As in the setting of the Prodigal son in Luke 15, everyone who has come to Jesus has come as an unprofitable servant. How did the Apostle Paul describe himself before being saved on the road to Damascus in 1 Timothy 1:15? He was a Chief of sinners.

3. a) Is there anyone on earth who, before knowing Jesus as his/her Lord and Savior, has been a "profitable" servant? No

b) Explain your answer using Romans 3:23.: All humans have sinned, and come short of the glory of God.

4. When Paul spoke of Onesimus being unprofitable and profitable, he was actually making a play on a word. The name "Onesimus" means profitable. Now that he was a Christian, Onesimus could live up to his name.:

a) In what way had Onesimus been unprofitable to Philemon? He was not a believer, inter-alia, he did something to him and run away.

b) In what way had Onesimus been profitable to Paul? He is now a believer and Brother in Christ.

When Paul first met Onesimus and found out that he was the runaway slave of a Christian he already knew from Colossae, he recognized that his heavenly Father was at work. He knew that God had guided and directed Onesimus' steps directly to Rome, to see him, for a specific purpose.

c) In what ways could Onesimus become profitable to Philemon? Onesimus was able to do a lot for Apostle Paul while in Prison, the same he will be able to do for Philemon and he is part of Paul.

Did you know the name "Onesimus" means profitable or useful? After Onesimus accepted Jesus as His personal Lord and Savior, he could live up to his name and be useful in ministry. And through the power of the gospel, God has made us useful again too.

5. Name another person whom Paul declared had been profitable and useful to his ministry. (2 Timothy 4:11): Mark

This was evidence of a restoration of trust in Mark from Paul. Previously, Paul had wanted nothing to do with him in Acts 15:36-40.

6. Since Paul was a Roman citizen, he knew very well what fate might be waiting for Onesimus upon his return. In verse 12, what did Paul ask Philemon to do with regard to Onesimus? to receive him, for now Onesimus is Paul's own bowels:

This was a volatile situation. Onesimus was a changed man, but he must have been nervous about going back to Philemon. After all Roman law gave slave owners the right to brand the forehead of runaway slaves, lock them in chains, or simply execute them. Onesimus knew he deserved any one of these punishments because he had not only run away from Philemon, but had stolen from him as well. Anything could happen.

7. What are some things Paul did as he made this request that would make it difficult for Philemon to disregard Paul's wishes regarding the fate of Onesimus?

a): He also addressed the letter to the entire Church to make it impossible
for Philemon to avoid.

b): He sent Onesimus back with someone.

8. In verse 12, how did Paul express further what Onesimus had meant to him? Onesimus was his own bowels:

9. Compare this description of his feelings with verse 17. Express how Paul felt about Onesimus in modern day language.: Apostle Paul is telling Philemon to see Onesimus as he sees him.

Do you see the parallel between Onesimus and ourselves?

Onesimus is such an obscure character in the Bible, but he perfectly exemplifies our salvation. Paul said he would pay whatever Philemon said was due to clear the debt for what Onesimus owed him. Although we should be punished for our sins, Jesus told his heavenly Father to charge those sins to Himself. Jesus paid for our sins on the cross so that we now can serve our God without fear of punishment.

Philemon 1:11-12 Commentary:

"11 (Formerly he was useless to you, but now he is indeed useful to you and to me. 12 I am sending him back to you, sending my very heart.)"

In these verses, the apostle Paul continues to address Philemon regarding Onesimus, highlighting the transformation that has taken place in Onesimus's life and expressing his intention to send Onesimus back to Philemon.

"Formerly he was useless to you, but now he is indeed useful to you and to me:" Paul contrasts Onesimus's former state with his current condition. The term "useless" likely refers not only to Onesimus's status as a runaway slave but also to his unproductive or negative behavior. The word "useful" reflects the transformation that has occurred in Onesimus's life through his encounter with the gospel and his relationship with Paul. This transformation has made Onesimus not only beneficial but also valuable to both Philemon and Paul.

"I am sending him back to you, sending my very heart:" Paul announces his intention to send Onesimus back to Philemon. The phrase "sending my very heart" demonstrates the depth of Paul's affection for Onesimus and his connection to him. This expression implies that Onesimus has become more than just a helper to Paul; he has become a beloved companion and an integral part of Paul's ministry.

Relevant Bible Verses:

1. Colossians 4:9 (ESV): "And with him Onesimus, our faithful and beloved brother, who is one of you. They will tell you of everything that has taken place here." - This verse from Colossians highlights Onesimus's transformation from being a runaway slave to becoming a faithful and beloved brother in Christ.

2. Ephesians 2:10 (ESV): "For we are his workmanship, created in Christ Jesus for good works, which God prepared beforehand, that we should walk in them." - This verse emphasizes the concept of transformation through Christ, as believers are created for good works.

3. Philemon 1:16 (ESV): "No longer as a bondservant but more than a bondservant, as a beloved brother—especially to me, but how much more to you, both in the flesh and in the Lord." - This verse echoes the transformation of Onesimus's identity from slave to beloved brother, reinforcing the theme of reconciliation and unity.

Key Themes and Implications:
1. Transformation and Redemption: These verses highlight the transformative power of the gospel. Onesimus's change from being "useless" to "useful" illustrates the potential for redemption and positive change that comes through a relationship with Christ.
2. Personal Connection: Paul's declaration that Onesimus is his "very heart" underscores the deep emotional bond that can develop among believers. It emphasizes the genuine and profound relationships that can be forged within the Christian community.
3. Restoration and Reconciliation: Paul's intention to send Onesimus back to Philemon reflects a desire for restoration and reconciliation. It demonstrates a commitment to resolving conflicts and fostering unity within the body of Christ.
4. Identity in Christ: Onesimus's transformation from a runaway slave to a beloved brother illustrates the new identity believers receive through faith in Christ. It reinforces the idea that our worth and value are grounded in our relationship with Him.

Personal Application:
1. Recognizing Transformation: Believers should acknowledge and celebrate the transformative work that Christ can bring about in individuals' lives, no matter their past.
2. Deep Relationships: Just as Paul developed a strong bond with Onesimus, believers can cultivate deep and meaningful relationships within the faith community.
3. Commitment to Reconciliation: The example of Paul's willingness to send Onesimus back to Philemon

encourages believers to actively seek restoration and reconciliation in their relationships.

4. Embracing New Identity: Reflecting on the transformation of Onesimus can remind believers of their own identity in Christ and encourage them to live out their new nature.

In conclusion, Philemon 1:11-12 highlights the profound transformation of Onesimus's life through his encounter with the gospel. These verses emphasize the themes of redemption, restoration, and the depth of relationships within the Christian community. Paul's intention to send Onesimus back to Philemon reflects his commitment to reconciliation and unity, setting the stage for the subsequent appeal for forgiveness and acceptance.

Study and Discussion Guide Verse 11-12:

1. How had becoming a Christian changed Onesimus? (vs. 11):

2. As in the setting of the Prodigal son in Luke 15, everyone who has come to Jesus has come as an unprofitable servant. How did the Apostle Paul describe himself before being saved on the road to Damascus in 1 Timothy 1:15?

3. a) Is there anyone on earth who, before knowing Jesus as his/her Lord and Savior, has been a "profitable" servant?

b) Explain your answer using Romans 3:23.:

4 When Paul spoke of Onesimus being unprofitable and profitable, he was actually making a play on a word. The name "Onesimus" means profitable. Now that he was a Christian, Onesimus could live up to his name.:

a) In what way had Onesimus been unprofitable to Philemon?

b) In what way had Onesimus been profitable to Paul?

c) In what ways could Onesimus become profitable to Philemon?

5. Name another person whom Paul declared had been profitable and useful to his ministry. (2 Timothy 4:11):

6. Since Paul was a Roman citizen, he knew very well what fate might be waiting for Onesimus upon his return. In verse 12, what did Paul ask Philemon to do with regard to Onesimus?

7. What are some things Paul did as he made this request that would make it difficult for Philemon to disregard Paul's wishes regarding the fate of Onesimus?

a):

b):

8. In verse 12, how did Paul express further what Onesimus had meant to him?

9. Compare this description of his feelings with verse 17. Express how Paul felt about Onesimus in modern day language.:

CHAPTER X

Do you think Paul would have retained Onesimus?

Philemon 1:13-14 Expositor's Study:

Philemon 13-14 13 whom I wished to keep with me, that on your behalf he might minister to me in my chains for the gospel. ¹⁴ But without your consent I wanted to do nothing, that your good deed might not be by compulsion, as it were, but voluntary.

Pursuant to verse 13, and in the event, there had not been this situation that needed to be set right, do you think Paul would have retained Onesimus with him?

I think Onesimus held on tightly to that letter to Philemon the whole way home. I imagine he never let the letter out of his sight. And it should be the SAME with our letter from God. The Bible is our standing assurance that what we believe is true. Though Satan has done his best to put us down, God saved us, set us free, and wrote a book about it to continually reassure us, "You're forgiven. You're saved. Now you belong to MY family."

Why had Paul refrained from doing what he wished?

According to the majority interpretation, Paul wrote this letter on behalf of Onesimus, a runaway slave who had wronged his owner Philemon. ... However, he considered it better to send him back to Philemon with an accompanying letter, which aimed to effect reconciliation between them as Christian brothers.

The price of a good servant in 60 AD was 500 denarii. Philemon would have had to spend that much (500 days wages) to buy a replacement when Onesimus ran away. In addition, there was the matter of the money which Onesimus had stolen. (Actually, this type of offence was so common in the ancient world that sometimes the words slave and thief were used interchangeably.) Very bleak picture, wasn't it?

And that is exactly the picture that you and I face apart from Christ! We, like Onesimus, have incurred a debt which cannot be paid. Without Jesus, men are in the exact same position before God that Onesimus was in before Philemon.

Paul's ethical principles from what we read in verse 14 are revealing that compulsion is not good leadership, but consideration for others is good leadership. Paul did not want to provide extrinsic motivation to Philemon to release Onesimus. He wanted Philemon to decide his own will.

Until I read this letter to Philemon, I didn't' realize what a talented leader Paul was. I knew he was a great theologian, an incredible author, a successful businessman (tentmaker) and church planter, and a compelling speaker.

But in this letter, we see his leadership skills as he competently addressed the situation. He left the decision completely up to Philemon, and didn't trample all over his rights as the slave's owner. And yet, as we see throughout this letter, Paul arranged things so it would be very difficult for Philemon to say no without losing face among his brothers and sisters in Christ.

Checking the New Testament only, how were masters to act, according to these verses?

a) Colossians 4:1: Masters, give unto your servants that which is just and equal; knowing that ye also have a Master in heaven.
b) Ephesians 6:9: And, ye masters, do the same things unto them, forbearing threatening: knowing that your Master also is in heaven; neither is their respect of persons with him.

Since slavery is no longer a part of our culture, we tend to skim over these passages. But in Greek culture, manual work was despised and the goal of being successful was getting to the point where you never had to do any work.

"It wasn't just menial tasks which were performed by slaves. Doctors, teachers, musicians, actors, secretaries, stewards were slaves. In fact, all the work of Rome was done by slaves. Roman attitude was that there was no point in being master of the world and doing one's own work. Let the slaves do that and let the citizens live in pampered idleness. The supply of slaves would never run out." (William Barclay, The Letters of James and Peter, The Westminster Press, 1976)
There was a cultural tendency to treat slaves as less than low class individuals. But in these passages, Christian masters were instructed not to abuse their power or their slaves.
The attributes of slaves as construed in other epistles of Paul.

a) Ephesians 6:5-8: 5 Servants, be obedient to them that are your masters according to the flesh, with fear and trembling, in singleness of your heart, as unto Christ; 6 Not with eyeservice, as men pleasers; but as the servants of Christ, doing the will of God from the heart; 7 With good will doing service, as to the Lord, and not to men: 8 Knowing that whatsoever good thing any man doeth, the same shall he receive of the Lord, whether he be bond or free.

b) Colossians 3:22-23: 22 Servants, obey in all things your masters according to the flesh; not with eyeservice, as men pleasers; but in singleness of heart, fearing God; 23 And whatsoever ye do, do it heartily, as to the Lord, and not unto men;

c) 1 Timothy 6:1: Let as many servants as are under the yoke count their own masters worthy of all honour, that the name of God and his doctrine be not blasphemed.

d) 1 Timothy 6:2: And they that have believing masters, let them not despise them, because they are brethren; but rather do them service, because they are faithful and beloved, partakers of the benefit. These things teach and exhort.

e) 1 Peter 2:18: Servants, be subject to your masters with all fear; not only to the good and gentle, but also to the froward.

f) Titus 2:9: Exhort servants to be obedient unto their own masters, and to please them well in all things; not answering again;

In the ancient world, Christians shocked the people of their time by mixing slaves and masters in the social setting of the church service. This meant that a slave might go to church and become an elder in the church, and actually serve in a position over his own master.

Philemon 1:13-14 Commentary:

"13 I would have been glad to keep him with me, in order that he might serve me on your behalf during my imprisonment for the gospel, 14 but I preferred to do nothing without your consent in order that your goodness might not be by compulsion but of your own accord."

In these verses, the apostle Paul continues his letter to Philemon, addressing the matter of Onesimus, Philemon's runaway slave who had become a believer and was now returning. Paul discusses his initial intention regarding Onesimus and reveals his thoughtful consideration for both Philemon's feelings and the principle of free will in their relationship.

Verse 13: "I would have been glad to keep him with me, in order that he might serve me on your behalf during my imprisonment for the gospel:"

- "I would have been glad to keep him with me:" Paul acknowledges his desire to have Onesimus stay with him, potentially to continue assisting him in his ministry while he is imprisoned.
- "in order that he might serve me on your behalf:" Paul clarifies that keeping Onesimus with him would have been beneficial for both of them. Onesimus's service to Paul could be seen as indirectly benefiting Philemon,

reinforcing the sense of partnership within the Christian community.

- "during my imprisonment for the gospel:" Paul's imprisonment is mentioned as the context for his consideration of Onesimus's assistance. Despite his own challenging circumstances, Paul is still thinking about how to fulfill his ministry.

Verse 14: "but I preferred to do nothing without your consent in order that your goodness might not be by compulsion but of your own accord:"

- "but I preferred to do nothing without your consent:" Paul emphasizes his commitment to respecting Philemon's authority and wishes. He refrains from making a unilateral decision regarding Onesimus's fate and instead values Philemon's input.
- "in order that your goodness might not be by compulsion but of your own accord:" Paul's decision is motivated by his desire for Philemon's response to be genuine and voluntary. He wants Philemon's actions to stem from a willing heart, reflecting true Christian virtue rather than coercion.

Relevant Bible Verses:

1. 2 Corinthians 9:7 (ESV): "Each one must give as he has decided in his heart, not reluctantly or under compulsion, for God loves a cheerful giver." - This verse aligns with Paul's desire for Philemon's goodness to be of his own accord and not compelled by external factors.

2. Matthew 6:1 (ESV): "Beware of practicing your righteousness before other people in order to be seen by them, for then you will have no reward from your Father who is in heaven." - Jesus teaches the importance of genuine, heart-felt actions rather than seeking recognition or praise from others.

3. Colossians 3:23-24 (ESV): "Whatever you do, work heartily, as for the Lord and not for men, knowing that from the Lord you will receive the inheritance as your reward. You are serving the Lord Christ." - The principle

of serving with sincerity and devotion, ultimately for the Lord's approval, is reflected in Paul's approach.

Key Themes and Implications:

1. Respect for Free Will: Paul's willingness to involve Philemon in the decision regarding Onesimus highlights the value of respecting free will and the importance of mutual agreement within the Christian community.
2. Genuine Goodness: Paul's emphasis on voluntary, uncoerced actions underscores the principle of genuine Christian virtue. Actions driven by a willing heart reflect a sincere commitment to Christ's teachings.
3. Partnership and Consideration: Paul's consideration of how Onesimus's service might benefit both him and Philemon underscores the interconnectedness and partnership among believers in their shared mission.

Personal Application:

1. Respecting Others: Believers should approach decisions and interactions with a respect for the free will and autonomy of others, seeking consensus and mutual agreement whenever possible.
2. Sincere Service: Like Paul, believers should engage in service and ministry with a genuine heart, motivated by a desire to honor Christ and contribute to the well-being of others.
3. Mutual Benefit: Consideration of how actions can mutually benefit individuals and the broader Christian community can lead to more meaningful and impactful service.
4. Authentic Virtue: Emulating Paul's approach encourages believers to cultivate authentic virtue that arises from a willing heart and a desire to please God rather than seeking recognition or reward from others.

In conclusion, Philemon 1:13-14 reveals Paul's thoughtful consideration for Philemon's feelings and his commitment to the principle of free will in their relationship. These verses highlight the themes of respect for autonomy, genuine goodness, and mutual benefit within the Christian community. Paul's approach serves as a model for believers in their interactions and decisions, encouraging them to cultivate authentic virtue and prioritize sincere service that honors Christ and respects the choices of others.

Study and Discussion Guide Verse 13-14:

1. If there had not been this situation that needed to be set right, what had Paul wished to do with Onesimus? (vs. 13):
2. Why had Paul refrained from doing what he wished?
3. What can be said about Paul's ethical principles from what we read in verse 14?
4. Checking the New Testament only, how were masters to act, according to these verses?
a) Colossians 4:1:
b) Ephesians 6:9:
5. How were slaves to perform, according to these verses?
a) Ephesians 6:5-8:
b) Colossians 3:22-23:
c) 1 Timothy 6:1:
d) 1 Timothy 6:2:
e) 1 Peter 2:18:
f) Titus 2:9:

CHAPTER XI

No Longer A Slave

Philemon 1:15-16 Expositor's Study:

Philemon 15-16 [15] For perhaps he departed for a while for this purpose, that you might receive him forever, [16] no longer as a slave but more than a slave—a beloved brother, especially to me but how much more to you, both in the flesh and in the Lord.

Onesimus has wronged Philemon, his master, and fled the area where he could not be punished by him. Further, when he came to Rome, he heard that Paul was incarcerated, and found him there. He knew Paul from his involvement in the churches of his home area. What Onesimus did not count on was that Paul would preach Jesus to him, and he would come to know Him as his Lord and Savior. He also did not know that Paul would instruct him to go back to Philemon! If he had suspected this before his visit, he would likely have not come to Paul in Rome. Even after he became a believer, this was an intimidating demand that Paul made.

However, the Bible doctrine and Theology of this is conspicuous. As impeccably exhibited in Romans 3:23, we are all sinners, alienated from God, and must be reconciled by Him. Perhaps we have been alienated from Him for a time on our life, so that He might receive us forever, inter-alia, there are several things that happen in our return. When we return to our God, coming by the blood of Jesus, these five things are accomplished.

In verse 15 we can see that this whole episode of the runaway slave is turning out for the good when Onesimus became a believer and was reconciled to his master Philemon. In contrast, the escape of Onesimus was nothing but trouble. It deprived Philemon of a worker and an asset. It made Onesimus a criminal, possibly subject to the death penalty. Yet in spite of all that, Paul could see that God had a purpose, and he wanted Philemon to see the purpose also. Romans 8:28

The infallible Word says that we are all sinners, alienated from God, and must be reconciled to Him.

What happened to Onesimus was sanctification. The idea behind the word sanctify is "to set apart" - to become something different and distinct, breaking old associations and forming a new association. God wants us to be set apart to Him for His use.

a) A work of ... (1 Thessalonians 5:23): Sanctification is a work of God the Father. "And the very God of peace sanctify you wholly" (I Thessalonians 5:23).

b) A work of ... (Ephesians 5:25-26): Sanctification is a work of God the Son. "Husbands, love your wives, even as Christ also loved the church, and gave himself for it; That he might sanctify and cleanse it with the washing of water by the word" (Ephesians 5:25-26).

c) A work of ... (2 Thessalonians 2:13): Sanctification is a work of God the Holy Spirit. "But we are bound to give thanks always to God for you, brethren beloved of the Lord, because God hath from the beginning chosen you to salvation through sanctification of the Spirit and belief of the truth" (II Thessalonians 2:13).

d) By the ... (John 17:17): Sanctification is by the Word of God. "Sanctify them through thy truth: thy word is truth" (John 17:17).

Sanctification is a progressive work of God and man that makes us more and more free from sin and more like Christ every day. There are no short cuts to sanctification. We must continually reach toward this goal, day after day, month after month, year after year. No one leaves this earth fully sanctified. There will always be more room for growth.

And I'm sure you've noticed this as well, the more I strive to line up this sinful flesh with the Word, the more I notice that needs improvement.

NO LONGER A SERVANT BUT A BROTHER BELOVED:

In verse 16 Paul brings it all into perspective. While Onesimus is a slave, the reality is something much bigger and more important than that. What does Paul mention about Onesimus in verse 16 that should convince Philemon to do the right thing? Onesimus is no longer a servant but a Brother Beloved. "Not now as a servant, but above a servant, a brother beloved, specially to me, but how much more unto thee, both in the flesh, and in the Lord?" (Philemon 16).

Onesimus ran away as a slave, but in what two ways did Paul ask Philemon to receive him back? (16-17):

a): Onesimus is now a brother beloved both in the flesh, and in the Lord. If a man is a stranger, I might make him my slave. But how can I make my brother be my slave? In this relationship as brothers and not slaves, Paul effectively abolished the sting of the "master-slave" relationship.

b): If Philemon count Apostle Paul a partner, then he should receive him (Onesimus) as he could as Apostle Paul. Here Paul was saying, "I am your partner in ministry work. We both strive to spread the gospel. Treat Onesimus as your partner in the Lord's work as well."

"All my state shall Tychicus declare unto you, who is a beloved brother, and a faithful minister and fellow servant in the Lord: Whom I have sent unto you for the same purpose, that he might know your estate, and comfort your hearts; With Onesimus, a faithful and beloved brother, who is one of you. They shall make known unto you all things which are done here" (Colossians 4:7-9).

"And say to Archippus, take heed to the ministry which thou hast received in the Lord, that thou fulfil it" (Colossians 4:17; compare with Philemon 2).

As we can see, Onesimus had been given a special recommendation by Paul, both in his letter to his master Philemon, and to the church in general, as the letter to the Colossians was to be read by the church in Laodicea as well. We can see that Philemon carried out the direction of Paul. Onesimus was no longer a slave. He was part of the family, and a trusted one, with the past left in the past.

There is a special place given to those who have offended our God, when they come to Him to be forgiven. He does exactly what He promises. "Old things are passed away; behold all things are become new" (II Corinthians 5:17). They are no longer aliens and foreigners. They are now the sons of God, and in His family. "Beloved, now are we the sons of God, and it doth not yet appear what we shall be: but we know that, when he shall appear, we shall be like him; for we shall see him as he is" (I John 3:2).

Philemon 1:15-16 Commentary:

"15 For this perhaps is why he was parted from you for a while, that you might have him back forever, 16 no longer as a bondservant but more than a bondservant, as a beloved brother—especially to me, but how much more to you, both in the flesh and in the Lord."

In these verses, the apostle Paul continues his plea to Philemon regarding Onesimus. He presents a perspective on the purpose behind Onesimus's departure and encourages Philemon to view Onesimus's return in a new light.

Verse 15: "For this perhaps is why he was parted from you for a while, that you might have him back forever:"

Paul offers a potential reason for Onesimus's separation from Philemon: to ultimately bring about a lasting and transformative reunion. This idea suggests that God's providence was at work in the circumstances, guiding the events toward a greater purpose.

Verse 16: "no longer as a bondservant but more than a bondservant, as a beloved brother—especially to me, but how much more to you, both in the flesh and in the Lord."

Paul contrasts Onesimus's former role as a bondservant with his new identity as a beloved brother in Christ. This transformation reflects the profound impact of the gospel on one's identity and relationships.

- "no longer as a bondservant:" Paul emphasizes that Onesimus's return is not merely a reinstatement of his former status as a slave. The gospel has brought about a radical change that transcends social norms and structures.
- "more than a bondservant:" By describing Onesimus as "more than a bondservant," Paul underscores the depth of transformation that has taken place. This transformation is not limited to superficial changes but encompasses a profound shift in identity and relationship.
- "as a beloved brother:" The use of the term "beloved brother" highlights the familial and spiritual bond that now exists between Philemon and Onesimus. This language reinforces the theme of unity and mutual love within the Christian community.
- "especially to me, but how much more to you:" Paul acknowledges his personal connection with Onesimus while urging Philemon to recognize the significance of their relationship as well. He emphasizes that their bond goes beyond a legal or social framework and is rooted in their shared faith in Christ.

Relevant Bible Verses:

1. Ephesians 2:19 (ESV): "So then you are no longer strangers and aliens, but you are fellow citizens with the saints and members of the household of God." - This verse aligns with the concept of believers being part of a spiritual family, united in Christ.

2. Galatians 3:28 (ESV): "There is neither Jew nor Greek, there is neither slave nor free, there is no male and female, for you are all one in Christ Jesus." - This verse emphasizes the unity and equality that believers share in Christ, transcending social distinctions.

3. Colossians 4:9 (ESV): "And with him Onesimus, our faithful and beloved brother, who is one of you. They will tell you of everything that has taken place here." - This verse reinforces the idea of Onesimus's transformed status as a beloved brother in Christ.

Key Themes and Implications:

1. Divine Providence: Paul suggests that Onesimus's separation from Philemon was not accidental but served a greater purpose. This perspective encourages believers to see God's guiding hand in all circumstances, even challenging ones.

2. Transformational Gospel: The transformation of Onesimus from a bondservant to a beloved brother illustrates the radical impact of the gospel on one's identity and relationships. It underscores the power of Christ's work to redefine and reshape lives.

3. Unity in Christ: The concept of beloved brotherhood highlights the unity and equality that believers share in Christ. It emphasizes the importance of viewing fellow believers through a lens of love and mutual respect.

4. Shift in Perspective: Paul invites Philemon to shift his perspective on Onesimus's return. Rather than focusing on legal or social categories, Philemon is encouraged to embrace Onesimus as a cherished member of the Christian community.

Personal Application:

1. Recognizing God's Purposes: Believers should seek to discern God's purposes even in challenging situations, trusting that He can use circumstances for greater good.

2. Identity in Christ: Onesimus's transformation encourages believers to embrace their identity as new creations in

Christ, experiencing a profound shift in their relationships and sense of belonging.

3. Embracing Unity: Just as Paul emphasizes unity between Philemon and Onesimus, believers should prioritize unity and mutual love within the body of Christ.

4. Transformational Relationships: The story of Onesimus underscores the potential for transformational relationships within the Christian community, where individuals experience profound changes through their connection to Christ.

In conclusion, Philemon 1:15-16 presents a perspective on the purpose behind Onesimus's departure and his transformed status upon his return. These verses underscore the themes of divine providence, transformation through the gospel, unity in Christ, and the power of shifting perspectives. Paul's appeal encourages Philemon to embrace Onesimus not as a mere bondservant but as a beloved brother, both in the flesh and in the Lord. This sets the stage for the ultimate appeal for forgiveness and reconciliation that follows in the letter.

Study and Discussion Guide Verse 15-16:

1. In what way was this whole episode of the runaway slave turning out for the good? (vs. 15):

2. The author of our text says that we are all sinners, alienated from God, and must be reconciled to Him. Briefly describe on your own words the five things that are accomplished when we return to God, coming by the blood of Jesus.:

a):

b):

c):

d):

e):

3. Sanctification is …

a) A work of … (1 Thessalonians 5:23):

b) A work of … (Ephesians 5:25-26):

c) A work of … (2 Thessalonians 2:13):

d) By the ... (John 17:17):

4. In verse 16 Paul brings it all into perspective. While Onesimus is a slave, the reality is something much bigger and more important than that. What does Paul mention about Onesimus in verse 16 that should convince Philemon to do the right thing?

 5. Onesimus ran away as a slave, but in what two ways did Paul ask Philemon to receive him back? (16-17):

a):

b):

CHAPTER XII

Philemon's Obedience Encouraged

Philemon 1:17 Expositor's Study:

Philemon 1:17 [17] If then you count me as a partner, receive him as you would me.

Philemon's Obedience Encouraged

As we can see, in verse 17 Apostle Paul is asking Philemon to receive Onesimus as a partner since Philemon and Paul were partners in Christ.

The logic of Paul's words was indisputable although the three men couldn't have been more different from one another. Paul was a working-class man - making tents for a living as well as preaching the gospel everywhere he travelled. Philemon was a wealthy Gentile and slaveowner. Onesimus was a runaway slave.

But all three were connected through their common allegiance to Christ, forcing them into an entirely new relationship where each acknowledged the other as one of God's adopted sons and a brother for whom Christ died. As such, they became partners and co-workers in this great commission to spread the gospel (Matthew 28:18-20).

What is the veracity of Paul's words in verse 17? Do you think Paul was really saying, "In other words, if you don't take him back … don't consider me your partner anymore"?

I think for Paul this was a deal breaker - he saw this situation as a testing of Philemon's faith. Was it real? This was certainly a critical moment for Philemon - he had to accept Onesimus as Paul requested or damage his testimony before the church members meeting in his own home.

Imagine what a positive impact such a radical departure from social convention would make on any doubtful eyes watching for his reaction - when Philemon recognized and honored Onesimus as Paul's substitute, and then welcomed him as though he were a spiritual partner like Paul within the very household where he once served as a slave.

Paul not only wrote to Philemon and the group meeting at his home, he also made recommendations on Onesimus' behalf to the church in general in Colossae. How did Paul describe Onesimus in his letter to the Colossians? (Colossians 4:9): a faithful and beloved brother, who is one of you. Paul could have referred to Onesimus as " ... that escaped slave whom I am sending back to his master." Instead, he called him a faithful and beloved brother, and let the Colossian Christians know that Onesimus was now one of them.

Instead of focusing on the wrong things Onesimus had done, Paul focused on the good. And God does the same. There is a special status given to those who have offended God, when they come to Him to be forgiven. How are they received? (2 Corinthians 5:17): Old things are passed away; behold, all things are become new. Becoming a new creation isn't just "turning over a new leaf" or "getting your act together." This is a gift from God received by faith. After a person receives the gift of becoming a new creation in Christ, he is challenged to live the life of a new creation (i.e., the process of sanctification).

Philemon 1:17 Commentary:

"So if you consider me your partner, receive him as you would receive me."

In this verse, the apostle Paul continues his appeal to Philemon regarding Onesimus, urging Philemon to extend the same hospitality and acceptance to Onesimus as he would to Paul himself. This statement emphasizes the depth of their relationship and the principles of unity and forgiveness within the Christian community.

"So if you consider me your partner:" Paul begins by referencing the close partnership he shares with Philemon. The term "partner" implies a deep and mutual relationship rooted in their shared faith and commitment to the gospel. This partnership carries weight and significance in Paul's appeal.

"receive him as you would receive me:" Paul's request to receive Onesimus is framed in a way that equates Onesimus's reception with the reception Paul would receive. This comparison underscores the importance of showing the same level of hospitality, warmth, and acceptance to Onesimus that one would show to an esteemed guest like Paul.

Relevant Bible Verses:

1. Matthew 10:40 (ESV): "Whoever receives you receives me, and whoever receives me receives him who sent me." - Jesus teaches the principle of receiving believers as representatives of Christ Himself. This verse underscores the significance of hospitality and acceptance within the context of faith.

2. Romans 15:7 (ESV): "Therefore welcome one another as Christ has welcomed you, for the glory of God." - This verse highlights the call for believers to welcome and accept one another, reflecting Christ's acceptance of us and bringing glory to God.

3. 3 John 1:8 (ESV): "Therefore we ought to support people like these, that we may be fellow workers for the truth." - This verse speaks to the importance of supporting fellow believers and working together for the sake of the truth, aligning with the concept of partnership.

Key Themes and Implications:

1. Unity and Hospitality: Paul's comparison between Onesimus and himself emphasizes the principle of unity and mutual acceptance within the Christian community. It encourages believers to extend the same level of hospitality to fellow believers as they would to esteemed leaders.

2. Representatives of Christ: The idea of receiving believers as representatives of Christ reflects the interconnectedness of the body of Christ. It underscores the importance of treating others with the same respect and honor we would show to Christ Himself.

3. Transformational Relationships: Paul's appeal highlights the transformative potential of relationships within the faith community. Onesimus's changed status and his reception by Philemon reflect the power of Christ's work to mend and restore relationships.

4. Stewardship of Unity: Believers are called to actively promote and maintain unity within the body of Christ. Receiving fellow believers with love and acceptance contributes to the well-being and strength of the faith community.

Personal Application:

1. Practicing Hospitality: Believers are encouraged to practice hospitality by welcoming and accepting fellow believers, treating them with the same respect and warmth they would show to Christ Himself.

2. Recognizing Unity: Paul's plea highlights the importance of recognizing the unity that exists among believers, regardless of social or cultural differences.

3. Modeling Christlikeness: Treating others with love and acceptance reflects the character of Christ and serves as a witness to the transformative power of the gospel.

4. Forgiveness and Reconciliation: The appeal to receive Onesimus mirrors the principles of forgiveness and reconciliation within the Christian faith. Believers should strive to mend broken relationships and foster unity.

In conclusion, Philemon 1:17 captures Paul's plea for Philemon to receive Onesimus with the same hospitality and acceptance that he would extend to Paul himself. This verse underscores the themes of unity, transformation, and the interconnectedness of believers within the body of Christ. Paul's appeal sets the stage for the culmination of his message, wherein he will make a direct request for forgiveness and reconciliation between Philemon and Onesimus.

Study and Discussion Guide Verse 17:

1. Upon what basis did Paul ask Philemon to receive Onesimus as he would Paul himself? (vs. 17):
 2. In verse 17, do you think Paul was really saying, "In other words, if you don't take him back … don't consider me your partner anymore"?
3. Paul not only wrote to Philemon and the group meeting at his home, he also made recommendations on Onesimus' behalf to the church in general in Colossae. How did Paul describe Onesimus in his letter to the Colossians? (Colossians 4:9):
4. Instead of focusing on the wrong things Onesimus had done, Paul focused on the good. And God does the same. There is a special status given to those who have offended God, when they come to Him to be forgiven. How are they received? (2 Corinthians 5:17):
5. The author of our text points out that, in the reconciliation between God and the sinner, there are several things we can notice.:
a) There is no ...:
b) There is no ...:
c) There is no ...:
d) There is no ...:

CHAPTER XIII

Paul's Promissory Note

Philemon 1:18-19 Expositor's Study:

Philemon 18-19 [18] But if he has wronged you or owes anything, put that on my account. [19] I, Paul, am writing with my own hand. I will repay—not to mention to you that you owe me even your own self besides.

PAUL'S PROMISSORY NOTE

What Is a Promissory Note?

A promissory note is a debt instrument that contains a written promise by one party (the note's issuer or maker) to pay another party (the note's payee) a definite sum of money, either on-demand or at a specified future date. A promissory note typically contains all the terms pertaining to the indebtedness, such as the principal amount, interest rate, maturity date, date and place of issuance, and issuer's signature.

Paul was offering to make good whatever financial or business losses Philemon had suffered as a result of Onesimus' behavior. While Paul owed Philemon nothing, even as Christ owes us nothing, he involved himself in Philemon's affairs by offering to pay Onesimus's debt, even as Christ (who knew no sin) took upon himself the sins of us all (Romans 5:6-11). Paul's involvement has a firm Christological basis.

"And all things are of God, who hath reconciled us to himself by Jesus Christ, and hath given to us the ministry of reconciliation; To wit, that God was in Christ, reconciling the world unto himself, not imputing their trespasses unto them; and hath committed unto us the word of reconciliation" ((II Corinthians 5:18-19). This is our word of reconciliation. He has done this for us, and we are to do this with others when they are accepted as the children of God.

Paul's promise to pay Onesimus' debt was made in the same spirit as Jesus' sacrifice, when He was willing to take our sin debt upon Himself and pay the price, even though He Himself had not incurred the debt. Hebrews 9:24-26: This was where Jesus put all our sin debt on His account, and it is the principle that Paul is using to require Philemon to take back his servant Onesimus, with a clean slate, forgiven, and never to have those charges brought up again. This is the doctrine of reconciliation in action. As God has done, so He requires of us. "And all things are of God, who hath reconciled us to himself by Jesus Christ, and hath given to us the ministry of reconciliation; To wit, that God was in Christ, reconciling the world unto himself, not imputing their trespasses unto them; and hath committed unto us the word of reconciliation" (II Corinthians 5:18-19). This is our word of reconciliation. He has done this for us, and we are to do this with others when they are accepted as the children of God.

Jesus' sacrifice was made on earth, but it is the basis for His continuing work as our mediator and High Priest in heaven.

Onesimus certainly owed a debt to Philemon. But in verse 19, Paul also reminded Philemon that he (Philemon) owed a debt to himself because it was, he (Paul) who had introducing him to his Savior Jesus. "I do not say to thee how thou owest unto me even thine own self besides" And here is the close of the appeal. Paul impeccably wants Philemon to take into consideration that it was him (Paul) who was responsible for taking him the Gospel, and introducing him (Philemon) to his Lord and Savior Jesus. This will place the position of Onesimus in perspective for Philemon. Jesus had accepted Philemon as His own, even though Philemon was a sinner and unworthy of His grace, in contrast, Philemon is to exercise that same grace with Onesimus, one whose crime rocked the life of Philemon. Whatever we receive from God will be required of us to bless others as we have been blessed.

According to verse 19, it is clear that Apostle Paul really knew Philemon. He knew him well enough to know just how far to "push the envelope" with him to make things right. In the normal circumstances, usually we think of the person who messes up as the one who needs to make it right. But here Paul is stressing that the one who had been wronged, Philemon, was the one who needed to take steps to make this right. Exhibit Matthew 18:21-22 [21] Then came Peter to him, and said, Lord, how oft shall my brother sin against me, and I forgive him? till seven times? [22] Jesus saith unto him, I say not unto thee, Until seven times: but, Until seventy times seven.

Behind Paul's offer is the awareness that he is Philemon's spiritual benefactor - that Philemon is obliged to Paul even as Onesimus is. Because of this, Paul believes his offer to pay Onesimus's costs should be canceled by Philemon's own debt (... you owe me your very self).

It is also implied in Paul's offer that Onesimus himself has satisfied his obligation to Philemon (and therefore paid his debt in full) by taking care of Paul's needs while in prison.

Philemon 1:18-19 Commentary:

"18 If he has wronged you at all, or owes you anything, charge that to my account. 19 I, Paul, write this with my own hand: I will repay it—to say nothing of your owing me even your own self."

In these verses, the apostle Paul continues his plea to Philemon regarding Onesimus, offering to take personal responsibility for any wrongs committed by Onesimus and for any debts owed to Philemon. Paul's willingness to bear the burden on Onesimus's behalf reflects the principles of forgiveness, reconciliation, and selflessness within the context of Christian relationships.

Verse 18: "If he has wronged you at all, or owes you anything, charge that to my account."

Paul makes an extraordinary offer to Philemon. If Onesimus has wronged Philemon in any way or has incurred any financial obligations, Paul volunteers to bear the responsibility for these actions. This demonstrates Paul's commitment to advocating for Onesimus's well-being and his desire to promote reconciliation between Philemon and Onesimus.

Verse 19: "I, Paul, write this with my own hand: I will repay it—to say nothing of your owing me even your own self."

- "I, Paul, write this with my own hand:" Paul's emphasis on writing with his own hand underscores the personal nature and sincerity of his offer. This gesture adds weight to his words, emphasizing his genuine willingness to take on any debts or wrongs.

- "I will repay it:" Paul assures Philemon that he is prepared to repay any debts or wrongs personally. This underscores Paul's commitment to accountability and reconciliation, as well as his deep concern for both Philemon and Onesimus.

- "to say nothing of your owing me even your own self:" Paul reminds Philemon of the spiritual debt he owes to Paul for his own conversion and growth in the faith. This gentle reminder serves as an additional incentive for Philemon to respond to Paul's plea with generosity and forgiveness.

Relevant Bible Verses:

1. Matthew 18:21-22 (ESV): "Then Peter came up and said to him, 'Lord, how often will my brother sin against me, and I forgive him? As many as seven times?' Jesus said to him, 'I do not say to you seven times, but seventy-seven times.'" - This teaching of Jesus underscores the principle

of forgiveness and reconciliation, which aligns with Paul's plea to Philemon.

2. Colossians 2:14 (ESV): "By canceling the record of debt that stood against us with its legal demands. This he set aside, nailing it to the cross." - The concept of Christ's cancellation of our debt of sin through His sacrifice aligns with Paul's offer to bear any debts owed by Onesimus.

3. Romans 5:8 (ESV): "But God shows his love for us in that while we were still sinners, Christ died for us." - Paul's willingness to take responsibility for Onesimus's actions reflects the sacrificial love and selflessness demonstrated by Christ's death on the cross.

Key Themes and Implications:

1. Forgiveness and Reconciliation: Paul's offer to bear any wrongs or debts on behalf of Onesimus demonstrates the principles of forgiveness and reconciliation that are central to the Christian faith. It models the kind of grace and mercy that believers are called to extend to one another.

2. Accountability and Restitution: Paul's willingness to take personal responsibility reflects the importance of being accountable for one's actions and making restitution for any wrongs committed. It emphasizes the concept of taking ownership of one's behavior.

3. Sacrificial Love: Paul's offer parallels the sacrificial love demonstrated by Christ's death on the cross for the forgiveness of sins. It highlights the selflessness and willingness to bear burdens for the well-being of others.

4. Debt of Gratitude: Paul reminds Philemon of the debt of gratitude he owes for his own spiritual growth and conversion. This serves as a gentle reminder of the interconnectedness of believers and the mutual support they provide.

Personal Application:

1. Forgiving Others: Believers are encouraged to emulate Paul's example by extending forgiveness and grace to those who have wronged them, even offering to bear the consequences on their behalf.

2. Taking Responsibility: When appropriate, believers should take responsibility for their actions and seek to make restitution for any wrongs they have committed.

3. Modeling Christ's Love: Paul's offer reflects the sacrificial love modeled by Christ. Believers should strive to demonstrate this selfless love in their relationships and interactions with others.

4. Remembering Gratitude: Reflecting on the debt of gratitude owed to Christ for salvation can inspire believers to extend similar grace and generosity to others.

In conclusion, Philemon 1:18-19 showcases Paul's remarkable willingness to take personal responsibility for any wrongs or debts associated with Onesimus. These verses underscore the themes of forgiveness, reconciliation, accountability, and sacrificial love within the context of Christian relationships. Paul's offer serves as a powerful example of the kind of selflessness and grace that believers are called to embody as they navigate relationships and seek unity within the body of Christ.

Study and Discussion Guide Verse 18-19:

1. From the text, it appears that Paul converted:
a) both_______ (vs. 19):
b) and ______ (vs. 10).:
2. What was Paul willing to do in behalf of Onesimus?
3. In verse 19, the words ______ are Paul's guarantee that if Philemon held these things against Onesimus, this was his bond that he would do what was promised above.:
4. Paul's promise to pay Onesimus' debt was made in the same spirit as Jesus' sacrifice, when He was willing to take our sin debt upon Himself and pay the price, even though He Himself had not incurred the debt. Explain this concept further using Hebrews 9:24-26:

5. Onesimus certainly owed a debt to Philemon. But in verse 19, Paul also reminded Philemon that he (Philemon) owed a debt to himself because it was he (Paul) who had:

6. It sounds like Paul really knew Philemon. He knew him well enough to know just how far to "push the envelope" with him to make things right. What is interesting is usually we think of the person who messes up as the one who needs to make it right. But here Paul is stressing that the one who had been wronged, ______ (who?), was the one who needed to take steps to make this right.:

CHAPTER XIV

Let Me Have Joy from You in the Lord

Philemon 1:20-21 Expositor's Study:

Philemon 20-21 [20] *Yes, brother, let me have joy from you in the Lord; refresh my heart in the Lord.* [21] *Having confidence in your obedience, I write to you, knowing that you will do even more than I say.*

There was nothing that gratifying Paul, and gave him more exultation, than that his fellow brethren followed God's perfect will. If Philemon could ever find a reason for this to be too difficult, he had only to rehearse the persecutions of Paul, who was writing while in incarceration, and had previously been stoned more than once, and had escaped death. He had been obedient to his Lord. His request of Philemon was much less difficult, as it did not require a risk of death. It required the death of his anger toward Onesimus

Do you think Philemon's forgiveness of Onesimus affect Paul (vs. 20) by giving him joy in the Lord and refresh his bowels in the Lord?

Earlier in the letter, Paul said that Philemon was a man who refreshed the heart of the saints (Philemon 7). Now, he specifically told Philemon how he could refresh Paul's heart and give him joy - by allowing Onesimus to stay with Paul.

There was nothing that pleased Paul more, or gave him more joy, than when his followers ... (vs. 21) do more than what he says. Obedience is not a popular word today, but Paul knew that obedience is a key part of our Christian walk.

In 1 John 2:3-6, the Apostle John sought to define the basics of commitment. What is the proof that one knows and loves the Lord? A statement of belief is insufficient. Words are cheap … nearly everyone claims to believe in Christ.:

a) The real test of faith in Christ (vs. 3) if we keep his commandments. It is impossible to obey God if a person doesn't really know Him. A believer's simple, loving obedience to God is the evidence that he knows Him.

 Although our old sinful flesh will rear its ugly head from time to time, especially with regard to habitual sin, as we move forward in the process of sanctification - our obedience will flow as a natural result of our fellowship with God.

b) If someone says that he knows Christ, but doesn't live for Him (vs. 4) then he is a liar, and the truth is not in him. Today there are a number of people who claim to be Christians but live flagrantly sinful lives. These people open Christianity to the world's mocking. Their pretense of being a Christian doesn't help the themselves, the Church, or the world. In fact, it can be quite damaging - as the image of the Church is tarnished, and those who don't know Jesus as their personal Savior may become hardened against the gospel message.

c) When a person keeps God's Word in his heart (vs. 5) it means the love of God is perfected in them and are in Him.

d) What should a person do to prove that he belongs to Christ? (vs. 6): He that saith he abideth in him ought himself also so to walk, even as he walked.

Jesus lived a completely sinless life and was always obedient to God's will while on earth. When we are abiding in Jesus, we must try to walk just as He walked - and live a life of obedience and love. Sin will not be completely eliminated in our lives until we come to glory, but our relationship to sin is changed when we pledge our hearts and lives to the Lord.

- A Christian no longer loves sin as he once did.
- A Christian no longer brags about his sin as he once did.
- A Christian no longer plans to sin as he once did.
- A Christian no longer fondly remembers his sin as he once did.
- A Christian never fully enjoys his sin as he once did.
- A Christian no longer is comfortable in habitual sin as he once was.

f) The real proof of one's faith is not what he says but what he does.

g) John 14:15 says, if you love Me, keep My commands. Notice Jesus didn't say, "If you keep My commands, I'll love you."

Before, we were living according to the world's standards of behavior - we tried to please our friends by acting as they do. After we have been forgiven, our relationship with Christ motivates us to behave in a different manner. Our motivation is changes from being a people-pleaser to doing our upmost to please and love God through our obedience.

Paul's request has now taken on a new dimension and become an even bigger challenge. Philemon (vs. 21) must be creative in the way he is to deal with Onesimus. If Paul expects him to do more, he must think of the ways of God, and apply them for himself, rather than wait for directions from Paul. We can start a thought in the mind of a believer, but there is a time when people must learn to think for themselves. This is what Philemon is facing.

I don't believe Onesimus expected to be accepted, given a home, and taken care of without giving back. He would have wanted to work for his living. So, I thought perhaps Philemon might have given Onesimus a better position upon his return, a promotion with more responsibility and status.

Paul's letter, full of appeal, was also full of hope. He knew that Philemon was not a bad or a harsh man. Paul had every reason to expect that Philemon would fulfill his Christian duty and more.

Philemon 1:20-21 Commentary:

"20 Yes, brother, I want some benefit from you in the Lord. Refresh my heart in Christ. 21 Confident of your obedience, I write to you, knowing that you will do even more than I say."

In these verses, the apostle Paul concludes his appeal to Philemon by expressing his hope for a positive response and outlining his expectations. He combines warmth, affirmation, and confidence in Philemon's obedience, framing his request within the context of their shared faith in Christ.

Verse 20: "Yes, brother, I want some benefit from you in the Lord. Refresh my heart in Christ."

- "Yes, brother:" Paul addresses Philemon as a brother in the faith, underscoring their mutual identity as members of the same spiritual family.

- "I want some benefit from you in the Lord:" Paul candidly expresses his desire for a specific favor or benefit from Philemon. This request is couched within the framework of their shared relationship with Christ, emphasizing their common faith and commitment.

- "Refresh my heart in Christ:" Paul's request goes beyond the material aspect; he seeks emotional and spiritual refreshment. He asks Philemon to respond in a way that will uplift and invigorate his own heart and spirit, invoking their shared bond in Christ.

Verse 21: "Confident of your obedience, I write to you, knowing that you will do even more than I say."

- "Confident of your obedience:" Paul expresses his assurance that Philemon will respond positively and obediently to his plea. This confidence is rooted in their shared faith and their history of partnership.

- "I write to you, knowing that you will do even more than I say:" Paul anticipates that Philemon's response will exceed his specific request. This statement reflects Paul's understanding of Philemon's character and his willingness to go above and beyond in his obedience.

Relevant Bible Verses:

1. Philippians 2:1-2 (ESV): "So if there is any encouragement in Christ, any comfort from love, any participation in the Spirit, any affection and sympathy, complete my joy by being of the same mind, having the same love, being in full accord and of one mind." - Paul's desire for unity and shared experience aligns with his request for benefit and refreshment from Philemon.

2. 2 Corinthians 9:7 (ESV): "Each one must give as he has decided in his heart, not reluctantly or under compulsion, for God loves a cheerful giver." - This principle of giving with a willing heart resonates with Paul's expectation of Philemon's response.

3. 1 Thessalonians 4:1 (ESV): "Finally, then, brothers, we ask and urge you in the Lord Jesus, that as you received from us how you ought to walk and to please God, just as you are doing, that you do so more and more." - The concept of continuous growth and exceeding expectations parallels Paul's anticipation of Philemon doing more than he asks.

Key Themes and Implications:

1. Mutual Identity: Paul's use of "brother" emphasizes the spiritual bond shared by believers. It reinforces the concept of unity and familial connection within the body of Christ.

2. Benefit and Refreshment: Paul's request for "benefit" and "refreshment" speaks to the emotional and spiritual support that believers can offer one another. It underscores the importance of nurturing and uplifting fellow believers.

3. Confidence in Obedience: Paul's confidence in Philemon's obedience reflects the trust and accountability present within Christian relationships. It encourages believers to honor their commitments and responsibilities.

4. Exceeding Expectations: Paul's expectation that Philemon will do "even more" reflects the principle of generosity and going beyond the minimum requirement. It encourages

believers to approach their service with enthusiasm and a willingness to surpass expectations.

Personal Application:

1. Fostering Unity: Believers are called to prioritize unity and mutual support within the faith community, providing emotional and spiritual benefit to one another.

2. Obedience and Trust: Demonstrating obedience and trust within Christian relationships builds a foundation of accountability and encourages others to respond positively.

3. Generous Giving: Paul's anticipation of Philemon's exceeding response highlights the principle of giving generously and with a willing heart. Believers should strive to go beyond minimum expectations in their acts of service.

4. Strengthening Hearts: Like Paul's request for refreshment, believers can play a role in uplifting and strengthening the hearts of fellow believers through their actions and words.

In conclusion, Philemon 1:20-21 reveals Paul's heartfelt desire for refreshment and benefit from Philemon, and his confidence in Philemon's obedience and willingness to exceed expectations. These verses underscore the themes of unity, mutual support, obedience, and generosity within the Christian community. Paul's appeal reflects his understanding of the depth of their relationship and his expectation that Philemon's response will reflect their shared commitment to Christ.

Study and Discussion Guide Verse 20-21:

1. How would Philemon's forgiveness of Onesimus affect Paul? (vs. 20):

2. There was nothing that pleased Paul more, or gave him more joy, than when his followers ... (vs. 21):

3. Obedience is not a popular word today, but Paul knew that obedience is a key part of our Christian walk. In 1 John 2:3-6, the Apostle John sought to define the basics of commitment. What is the proof that one knows and loves the Lord? A statement of belief is insufficient. Words are cheap ... nearly everyone claims to

believe   in   Christ.:

a) What is the real test of my faith in Christ? (vs. 3):

b) What if someone says that he knows Christ, but doesn't live for Him? (vs. 4):

c) What happens when a person keeps God's Word? (vs. 5):

d) What should a person do to prove that he belongs to Christ? (vs. 6):

e) The real proof of one's faith is not what he says but what he _____:

f) John 14:15 says, If you love Me, My commands. Notice Jesus didn't say, "If you keep My commands, I'll love you.":

4. Paul's request has now taken on a new dimension and become an even bigger challenge. What are some things Philemon might do to fulfill Paul's expectation that, " … knowing that you will do even more than I say?" (vs. 21):

CHAPTER XV

Paul's Request

Philemon 1:22 Expositor's Study:

Philemon 1:22 [22] *But, meanwhile, also prepare a guest room for me, for I trust that through your prayers I shall be granted to you.*

In addition to appealing for Onesimus, Paul requested of Philemon in verse 22 to:

a): Prepare a lodging for him.

This showed the close relationship between Paul and Philemon. Paul knew there would always be a room available for him at Philemon's home. Obviously, Paul expected to be released from prison in the near future.

Paul remained in Rome for at least two years (Acts 28:30), where, despite being a prisoner, he wrote a very large part of what we now have as the New Testament - the epistles to the Ephesians, Philippians, Colossians, Philemon, and possibly Hebrews.

Although the Bible doesn't say, most scholars believe that he was eventually acquitted of the charges and released in 63 or 64 A.D., and then he made his way back through Greece and Asia Minor (Turkey) before again being arrested and returned to Rome where he was martyred about 67 A.D., during the time of Emperor Nero.
b): Pray for him and given to him

Yes. Paul wanted Philemon to pray, and he didn't think of the prayers as a mere formality. Paul believed that it would be through the prayers of Philemon that he would be released and they could get together again.

Have you ever said to someone, "I'll be praying for you about this," and then promptly forgot to do it? Then when we see that person next, we remember that we forgot to pray for them, but lie and say, 'Oh, I've been praying for you. How are things going?" How sad that we feel we must lie about something as sacred and holy as prayer to save face.

If this is something you have done in the past, there are some easy fixes for this, especially with the technology we have today.

- When someone asks for prayer, do it right then. You might pray with them, or pray as you're walking away.
- Be honest. If you're busy and can't pray right then, you could say, "Text me a reminder to pray about this." Or, "Send me an email, so I won't forget about this."
- Create a prayer list in your Smart Phone, and make a quick note right then.
- Don't be a Pharisee. Sometimes we make promises of prayer because we want to be liked by the person making the request. Either don't promise at all, or be sure to make good on the promise.

If Philemon had a thought about disregarding all the instructions Paul had given, this would have changed his mind. Paul was actually planning to come in the flesh, and see what all had been done. That could have been a dreaded day if God's will have had not been accomplished, inter-alia, I see this as a not-so-subtle encouragement that Philemon should fulfill Paul's request.

Paul trusted that through Philemon's prayers he shall be given unto him as exhibited in verse 22.

Philemon 1:22 Commentary:

"At the same time, prepare a guest room for me, for I am hoping that through your prayers I will be graciously given to you."

In this verse, the apostle Paul adds a personal request to his message to Philemon. He asks Philemon to prepare a guest room for him, expressing his desire to visit Philemon and the Colossian church. Paul's request is accompanied by a mention of his hope that his visit will be facilitated through the prayers of the believers.

"At the same time, prepare a guest room for me:" Paul's request for a guest room reflects his intention to visit Philemon in person. This indicates his desire for continued fellowship and partnership with Philemon and the local church.

"for I am hoping that through your prayers I will be graciously given to you:" Paul's hope for his visit is grounded in the power of prayer. He acknowledges the potential for God's grace to be manifested through the prayers of the believers, resulting in the realization of his desire to visit.

Relevant Bible Verses:

1. Romans 15:24 (ESV): "I hope to see you in passing as I go to Spain, and to be helped on my journey there by you, once I have enjoyed your company for a while." - This verse from Romans shows Paul's desire for personal interaction with fellow believers and his hope to receive assistance from them.

2. Colossians 4:3 (ESV): "At the same time, pray also for us, that God may open to us a door for the word, to declare the mystery of Christ, on account of which I am in prison." - Paul's emphasis on prayer aligns with his request for Philemon's prayers. It highlights the importance of seeking God's guidance and intervention through prayer.

3. 1 Thessalonians 5:25 (ESV): "Brothers, pray for us." - Paul's frequent request for prayer underscores the

significance of intercessory prayer within the Christian community.

Key Themes and Implications:

1. Fellowship and Partnership: Paul's request for a guest room indicates his desire for ongoing fellowship and partnership with Philemon and the Colossian church. It reflects the importance of personal connections and collaboration within the body of Christ.

2. Importance of Prayer: Paul's mention of his hope being realized through the prayers of the believers highlights the power of prayer in shaping outcomes and facilitating God's will.

3. Anticipation of God's Grace: Paul's mention of being "graciously given" suggests an attitude of humility and reliance on God's providence. It reflects a willingness to submit his plans to God's guidance and timing.

Personal Application:

1. Hospitality and Fellowship: Believers should be open to extending hospitality and fellowship to fellow believers, fostering a sense of community and support.

2. Prayerful Anticipation: Paul's expectation of his visit being facilitated through prayer encourages believers to approach their plans and desires with a posture of prayerful reliance on God's guidance.

3. Humility and Submission: Paul's acknowledgment of being "graciously given" highlights the importance of humility and submission to God's will, recognizing that outcomes are ultimately determined by His providence.

4. Interconnectedness: The request for prayer and the hope for a visit underscore the interconnectedness of believers and the impact of their actions and prayers on one another's lives.

In conclusion, Philemon 1:22 reveals Paul's personal request for a guest room and his hope for a visit to Philemon. This verse emphasizes the themes of fellowship, prayer, humility, and interconnectedness within the Christian community. Paul's anticipation of his visit being facilitated through prayer serves as a reminder of the importance of seeking God's guidance and relying on His grace in all aspects of life and relationships.

Study and Discussion Guide Verse 22:

1. In addition to appealing for Onesimus, what two other things did Paul request of Philemon in verse 22?
a):
b):
2. If Philemon had any thoughts about disregarding the requests Paul had made, how might Paul's request for lodging have tactfully induced Philemon to honor his request for Onesimus?
3. What did Paul trust would be the result of Philemon's prayer for him? (vs. 22):
4. The author of our text says that we have the same commission that Philemon had from Paul – to do even more than we are asked. For example:
a) In Malachi 3:10, we are told to bring our tithes into the storehouse. But we could also ...:
b) In Mark 12:31 we are told to love your neighbor as yourself, but in Mathew 25:35-40, we are encouraged to also ...:
c) In Matthew 18:21, we are told to forgive people who have harmed us in any way. But in Matthew 5:44, we are told to go beyond forgiveness and also …:

CHAPTER XVI

Who Else Sent Greetings to Philemon and the Church?

Philemon 1:23-24 Expositor's Study:

Philemon 1:23-24 [23] Epaphras, my fellow prisoner in Christ Jesus, greets you, [24] as do Mark, Aristarchus, Demas, Luke, my fellow laborers.

Who else sent greetings to Philemon and the church? (vs. 23-24):

Epaphras and Demas. The Demas mentioned here is probably the same person mentioned in 2 Timothy 4:10, who left the ministry because he loved "this present world." At one time Demas was devoted to the ministry. He was passionate about the cause of Jesus Christ! In the beginning he was willing to face the persecutions that came with the position.

Demas' leaving the ministry doesn't necessarily imply that he had turned to the sinful pleasures of this world. It's more likely that he left because he didn't want to take a chance on dying because of the persecution they would be facing. Demas chose security and safety over devotion, determination and the possibility of death.

This problem of people leaving their God-appointed positions still exists today. Studies show that around 1,500 ministers are leaving the ministry each month. In addition, there are countless people who have simply quit serving at church - whether it's teaching a class, playing an instrument, or serving on a committee. The most common excuses are ... " I'm too busy," and " I'm burnt out."

Which of these men in verse 24 also wrote books of the New Testament?

a): Mark. At one time, Paul had refused to take Mark along on a journey. On an earlier journey, Mark had not gone any further than Perga, in Pamphylia. Instead, he had left the ministry to go back home to his mother in Jerusalem (Matthew 10:37). Some commentaries say he left because he was sick - others say he was just homesick.

However, here we see the attitude of Paul against Mark had turned around. Paul was not only reconciled with Mark, but he was including him in his greetings to Philemon and the church.

John Mark was converted by Peter, and is the author of the Gospel of Mark, given by divine inspiration. What if Paul had not been forgiving of Mark's original lack of maturity? In that case, Mark - feeling rejected - might have rejected the faith of such hard-nosed people, and never have written this anointed Gospel!

b): Luke. Luke was a Gentile and is the only non-Jewish New Testament writer. The date and circumstances of his conversion are unknown. According to his own statement (Luke 1:2), he was not an "eye-witness and minister of the word from the beginning." He was a physician (Colossians 4:14), and Paul's companion on several mission trips.

Which of these men who sent greetings with Paul to Philemon do we also find in each of the following verses?
a) Colossians 4:10-14: Epaphras
b) Colossians 1:7; 4:12,13: Epaphras,

Epapras was a faithful Christian and founder of the Church at Colossae.

c) Acts 12:12,25; 13:5,13; 15:36-40; 2Ti 4:11; 1Pe 5:13: Mark
d) Acts 19:29; 20:4; 27:2: Gaius
e) 2 Timothy 4:10: Titus
f) 2 Timothy 4:11: Luke

By listing these names, Paul had put Philemon in an inescapable position. There was now a great number of believers who knew the full story about Philemon and Onesimus.

Philemon would have some tall explaining to do if Paul were to find out from the witnesses that Onesimus had been killed or treated badly.

In everything we do, we cannot escape the fact that we are not alone, and our actions are being watched by others. What do we learn regarding this in the following verses?

a) Hebrews 12:1: Therefore, since we are surrounded by such a great cloud of witnesses, let us throw off everything that hinders and the sin that so easily entangles. And let us run with perseverance the race marked out for us,

b) 1 Peter 2:11-12: 11 Dear friends, I urge you, as foreigners and exiles, to abstain from sinful desires, which wage war against your soul. 12 Live such good lives among the pagans that, though they accuse you of doing wrong, they may see your good deeds and glorify God on the day he visits us.

c) 1 Corinthians 8:9, Romans 14:13: Be careful, however, that the exercise of your rights does not become a stumbling block to the weak.; Therefore, let us stop passing judgment on one another. Instead, make up your mind not to put any stumbling block or obstacle in the way of a brother or sister.

There are two ways we can cause our brother to stumble or fall.

- We can discourage or beat them down by using legalism against them.
- We can do it by enticing them to sin through an unwise use of our own liberty.

d) 1 Timothy 4:12: Don't let anyone look down on you because you are young, but set an example for the believers in speech, in conduct, in love, in faith and in purity.

e) Titus 2:7: In everything set them an example by doing what is good. In your teaching show integrity, seriousness.

Titus had to be more than a teacher, he also had to be an example. His guidance to others would not be taken seriously if he himself was not walking worthy of the calling.

Philemon 1:23-24 Commentary:

"23 Epaphras, my fellow prisoner in Christ Jesus, sends greetings to you, 24 and so do Mark, Aristarchus, Demas, and Luke, my fellow workers."

In these verses, the apostle Paul concludes his letter to Philemon by sending greetings from several individuals who are closely connected to his ministry. These greetings reveal the sense of community and partnership that existed among Paul and his fellow workers.

Verse 23: "Epaphras, my fellow prisoner in Christ Jesus, sends greetings to you:"

- "Epaphras:" Epaphras was a faithful co-worker of Paul, likely a native of Colossae. He is mentioned in the context of Paul's imprisonment, suggesting that he may have been a fellow prisoner for the sake of the gospel or that he was ministering alongside Paul during his imprisonment.

- "my fellow prisoner in Christ Jesus:" The term "fellow prisoner" indicates not only a shared physical circumstance but also a shared commitment to the gospel. This emphasizes the sacrificial nature of their ministry and their willingness to suffer for the sake of Christ.

Verse 24: "and so do Mark, Aristarchus, Demas, and Luke, my fellow workers:

- "Mark:" Mark, also known as John Mark, was a cousin of Barnabas and a fellow worker in Paul's ministry. He was involved in the early spread of the gospel and is believed to be the author of the Gospel of Mark.

- "Aristarchus:" Aristarchus was a Macedonian from Thessalonica who accompanied Paul on his missionary journeys. He is mentioned as a fellow prisoner and a companion of Paul during various stages of his ministry.

- "Demas:" Demas is mentioned here as a fellow worker, but his later departure from Paul's ministry is noted in 2 Timothy 4:10. This highlights the complexity of human relationships and the challenges faced by early Christian leaders.
- "Luke:" Luke, the author of the Gospel of Luke and the book of Acts, is mentioned as a fellow worker of Paul. He traveled with Paul on several missionary journeys and played a significant role in recording the early history of the Christian church.

Relevant Bible Verses:

1. Colossians 1:7 (ESV): "Just as you learned it from Epaphras our beloved fellow servant. He is a faithful minister of Christ on your behalf."
2. Colossians 4:10 (ESV): "Aristarchus my fellow prisoner greets you, and Mark the cousin of Barnabas (concerning whom you have received instructions—if he comes to you, welcome him)."
3. 2 Timothy 4:10 (ESV): "For Demas, in love with this present world, has deserted me and gone to Thessalonica. Crescens has gone to Galatia, Titus to Dalmatia."
4. Colossians 4:14 (ESV): "Luke the beloved physician greets you, as does Demas."

Key Themes and Implications:

1. Community and Partnership: These verses emphasize the strong sense of community and partnership that existed among early Christian workers. They worked together, faced challenges together, and supported one another in their shared mission.
2. Sacrifice and Suffering: The mention of Epaphras as a fellow prisoner highlights the sacrificial nature of their ministry. It serves as a reminder of the challenges and hardships that early believers willingly endured for the sake of the gospel.

3. Complex Relationships: The inclusion of Demas, who later deserted Paul, serves as a reminder of the complexities and human frailties present even among those who were actively involved in spreading the gospel.

4. Collaborative Ministry: The mention of these individuals as "fellow workers" underscores the collaborative nature of early Christian ministry. Each person contributed their unique skills and gifts to advance the kingdom of God.

Personal Application:

1. Community and Support: Believers today should prioritize community and partnership in their service to God. Working together and supporting one another in ministry can lead to greater effectiveness and impact.

2. Sacrificial Service: The example of Epaphras and others highlights the willingness to endure hardships and sacrifices for the sake of the gospel. Believers should be willing to serve sacrificially, even if it involves personal challenges.

3. Humility and Forgiveness: The presence of Demas, who later deserted, serves as a reminder of the need for humility, forgiveness, and understanding in dealing with the imperfections of fellow believers.

4. Utilizing Gifts: Just as these individuals had unique roles and gifts in early Christian ministry, believers today should recognize and utilize their own gifts to contribute to the advancement of the kingdom of God.

In conclusion, Philemon 1:23-24 offers a glimpse into the close-knit community and collaborative ministry of Paul and his fellow workers. The inclusion of these individuals' greetings reflects the themes of partnership, sacrifice, and the complexities of human relationships within the context of early Christian ministry. The example of these early workers encourages believers to cultivate strong relationships, serve sacrificially, and utilize their gifts for the greater mission of spreading the gospel.

Study and Discussion Guide Verse 23-24:

1. Who else sent greetings to Philemon and the church? (vs. 23-24):

2. Which of these men also wrote books of the New Testament?

a):

b):

3. Which of these men who sent greetings with Paul to Philemon do we also find in each of the following verses?

a) Colossians 4:10-14:

b) Colossians 1:7; 4:12,13:

c) Acts 12:12,25; 13:5,13; 15:36-40; 2Ti 4:11; 1Pe 5:13: Mark

d) Acts 19:29; 20:4; 27:2:

e) 2 Timothy 4:10:

f) 2 Timothy 4:11:

4. By listing these names, Paul had put Philemon in an inescapable position. There was now a great number of _______ who knew the full story about Philemon and Onesimus.:

5. In everything we do, we cannot escape the fact that we are not alone, and our actions are being watched by others. What do we learn regarding this in the following verses?

a) Hebrews 12:1:

b) 1 Peter 2:11-12:

c) 1 Corinthians 8:9, Romans 14:13:

d) 1 Timothy 4:12:

e) Titus 2:7:

CHAPTER XVII

Paul's Final Prayer

Philemon 1:25 Expositor's Study:

Philemon 1:25 [25] *The grace of our Lord Jesus Christ be with your spirit. Amen.*

Paul's final prayer in verse 25 of this epistle is the grace of the Lord Jesus Christ be with your spirit.

Paul did not say this to simply fill up space at the end of his letter. To him, the Christian life begins and ends with the grace of our Lord Jesus Christ, so it was appropriate that his letters began and ended with grace also. Compare this to Paul's greeting in verse 3.

a) What is the same? Grace and peace to you from Lord Jesus Christ.

b) What is different? God our Father [In verse 3, Paul mentioned the Father]

Furthermore, "peace." In those days, "peace" was a typical Jewish greeting (Judges 19:20), but until we know and appropriate grace, we can't experience peace. By including both of these two words in so many of his salutations and closings, Paul placed a strong emphasis and focus on these two unmerited blessings given to believers in Christ Jesus.

These last words of Paul reflect a man who deeply loved Jesus and had received His grace. Paul's appreciation and thanks for such undeserved mercy and grace marked his entire ... (Thought question – answers will vary

This was a common blessing Paul used to close his letters. Variations on this blessing can be found in Galatians 6:18, Philippians 4:23, and 2 Timothy 4:22, In the original language, the plural form of the noun "you" was always used, showing the message was intended for the entire church as well as the person to whom the epistle may have been addressed. Grace is the highest blessing we could pray for anyone.:

a) What is grace? (Ephesians 2:8-10): it is the gift of God.

b) How do we receive saving grace? (Romans 10:9-11): If you declare with your mouth, "Jesus is Lord," and believe in your heart that God raised him from the dead, you will be saved.

Intellectual agreement with the facts of the cross and the resurrection is not enough. You must believe in your heart, but even that belief is not enough without accompanying action of confessing with your mouth.

c) Grace is always accompanied by ... (1 Timothy 1;14): with the faith and love that are in Christ Jesus.

d) After we have been saved, sin will not be our master anymore, because we are not under law, but under grace. (Romans 6:14).

Paul knew that what he wrote to Philemon was worthy to be agreed with, so he added the final word of agreement (vs. 25) spirit [The grace of the Lord Jesus Christ be with your spirit.]

We come to the end of a masterfully written letter. In his writing, Paul tugged at the heartstrings, leaned heavily on a Christian's faith and forgiveness, and trusted heavily in the value of a relationship between two men, Paul and Philemon.

Like Paul, we should always appeal to others to do what is right. God has called us to a life of doing the right thing in our own relationships with others. We should endeavor to motivate others by handling our own affairs properly and with love, and by appealing to others verbally when a situation come to our attention.

Whether Onesimus was needed in Rome is not important. The most important part of this is that Philemon had a need to exercise the grace that had been given to him by Jesus, and Onesimus was in need of seeing the exercise of grace in a practical way by a believer.

Philemon 1:25 Commentary:

"The grace of the Lord Jesus Christ be with your spirit."

This brief concluding verse of the Book of Philemon contains a heartfelt blessing and prayer for Philemon. It underscores the central theme of grace and encapsulates the essence of the Christian faith—relying on the grace of Jesus Christ.

"The grace of the Lord Jesus Christ be with your spirit:"

- "The grace of the Lord Jesus Christ:" The reference to "grace" highlights the unmerited favor and divine blessing that comes through Jesus Christ. Grace is at the heart of the gospel message, representing God's love, forgiveness, and salvation freely given to believers.

- "be with your spirit:" This phrase suggests a desire for the presence and work of God's grace to be experienced deeply and personally within Philemon's inner being, encompassing his thoughts, emotions, and spiritual life.

Relevant Bible Verses:

1. 2 Corinthians 13:14 (ESV): "The grace of the Lord Jesus Christ and the love of God and the fellowship of the Holy Spirit be with you all." - Similar to Philemon 1:25, this verse emphasizes the triune nature of God and invokes His grace upon believers.

2. Galatians 6:18 (ESV): "The grace of our Lord Jesus Christ be with your spirit, brothers. Amen." - This verse echoes the same sentiment as Philemon 1:25, underscoring the importance of God's grace in the lives of believers.
3. Ephesians 6:24 (ESV): "Grace be with all who love our Lord Jesus Christ with love incorruptible." - The connection between grace and love is emphasized here, suggesting that grace is experienced through a genuine love for Christ.

Key Themes and Implications:
1. Central Role of Grace: The verse highlights the significance of God's grace in the Christian faith. Grace is the foundation of salvation, reconciliation, and transformation, and it serves as a constant reminder of God's unending love and mercy.
2. Personal Blessing: The prayer for grace to be with Philemon's spirit reflects the intimate and personal nature of the Christian walk. It acknowledges the role of grace in shaping one's inner thoughts, attitudes, and spiritual growth.
3. Trinitarian Blessing: While not explicitly stated, the reference to the "Lord Jesus Christ" echoes the Trinitarian understanding of God, suggesting that the blessing encompasses the work of the Father, the Son, and the Holy Spirit.

Personal Application:
1. Grace-Centered Perspective: Believers should approach life with a grace-centered perspective, recognizing their need for God's grace and relying on it for daily living and growth.
2. Inner Transformation: The prayer for grace to be with one's spirit encourages believers to seek inner transformation and renewal through the work of the Holy Spirit.
3. Triune Blessing: Recognizing the triune nature of God, believers can seek the fullness of God's presence—Father, Son, and Holy Spirit—in their lives.

4. Living in Grace: Just as Philemon was blessed with the desire for grace to be with him, believers should actively seek to live in the reality of God's grace, extending it to others as well.

In conclusion, Philemon 1:25 concludes the letter with a heartfelt prayer for the grace of the Lord Jesus Christ to be with Philemon's spirit. This verse encapsulates the essence of the Christian faith by emphasizing the centrality of grace and its transformative power. It serves as a reminder that believers are recipients of God's unmerited favor and are called to live in the abundance of His grace.

Shalom,

Dr. Maxwell Shimba

Study and Discussion Guide Verse 25:

1. What was Paul's final prayer in verse 25 of this epistle?
2. Paul did not say this to simply fill up space at the end of his letter. To him, the Christian life begins and ends with the grace of our Lord Jesus Christ, so it was appropriate that his letters began and ended with grace also. Compare this to Paul's greeting in verse 3?
a) What is the same?
b) What is different?
3. These last words of Paul reflect a man who deeply loved Jesus and had received His grace. Paul's appreciation and thanks for such undeserved mercy and grace marked his entire … (Thought question – answers will vary.):
4. This was a common blessing Paul used to close his letters. Variations on this blessing can be found in Galatians 6:18, Philippians 4:23, and 2 Timothy 4:22, In the original language, the plural form of the noun "you" was always used, showing the message was intended for the entire church as well as the person to whom the epistle may have been addressed. Grace is the highest blessing we could pray for anyone.:
a) What is grace? (Ephesians 2:8-10):
b) How do we receive saving grace? (Romans 10:9-11
c) Grace is always accompanied by ... (1 Timothy 1;14): d) After we have been saved, sin will not be our master anymore, because we are not under law, but under ... (Romans 6:14).:
5. Paul knew that what he wrote to Philemon was worthy to be agreed with, so he added the final word of agreement ... _______ (vs. 25).:

CONCLUSION

Based on our knowledge regarding Philemon's position in the church and Paul's friendship with him, Philemon treated Onesimus as a brother in the Lord and no longer a running slave.

Forgiveness is a prominent theme in the Bible. Yet, it's not uncommon for Christians to have trouble forgiving people who have hurt them. The act of forgiving doesn't come easy for most of us. Our natural instinct is to recoil in self-protection when we've been injured. We don't naturally overflow with mercy, grace and understanding when we've been wronged.

But forgiveness is a choice we make through a decision of our will (whether we're feeling it or not), motivated by obedience to God and His command to forgive.

That is certainly not the way the world thinks. However, in Luke 6:30, Jesus said, " Give to every man that asketh of thee; and of him that taketh away thy goods ask them not again." He is saying, " If someone takes what is yours, don't insist on getting it back."

We forgive by faith, out of obedience. Since forgiveness goes against our nature, we must forgive by faith, whether we feel like it or not. We must trust God to do the work in us that needs to be done so that the forgiveness will be complete.

I believe God honors our commitment to obey Him and our desire to please him when we choose to forgive. He completes the work in His time. We must continue to forgive by faith (our part), until the work of forgiveness (the Lord's part), is done in our hearts. "Being confident of this very thing, that he which hath begun a good work in you will perform it until the day of Jesus Christ" (Philippians 1:6).

NOTES

www.ingramcontent.com/pod-product-compliance
Lightning Source LLC
Chambersburg PA
CBHW061315120726

48001CB00002B/516